PARADISE GARDENS

PARADISE GARDENS

The world's most beautiful Islamic gardens

MONTY DON & DERRY MOORE

TWO ROADS

Contents

10   Introduction

16   I R A N

20   Pasargadae, Fars

24   Bagh-e Fin, Kashan

34   The Maidan (Naqsh-e Jahan), Isfahan

40   Chehel Sotoun, Isfahan

46   Hasht Behest, Isfahan

52   Bagh-e Eram, Shiraz

60   I N D I A

66   Lodi Gardens, Delhi

72   Humayun's Tomb, Delhi

80   Amber Palace, Jaipur

88   Akbar's Tomb, Sikandra

94   Taj Mahal, Agra

100   Shalimar Bagh, Kashmir

106   Nishat Bagh, Kashmir

112   Pari Mahal, Kashmir

114   Samode Bagh, Jaipur

TITLE PAGE
A glimpse into a courtyard in the Urquijo Garden, Toledo.

120   MOROCCO

124   Agdal, Marrakech

128   The Chellah, Rabat

132   Palais Lamrani Riad, Marrakech

136   Le Jardin Secret, Marrakech

144   Umberto Pasti Garden, Tangier

148   Le Jardin Majorelle, Marrakech

158   SPAIN

162   The Alhambra, Granada

172   Real Alcázar, Seville

180   Urquijo Garden (Palacio de Galiana), Toledo

188   TURKEY

192   Topkapi Palace, Istanbul

200   Emirgan Park, Istanbul

204   ENGLAND

208   Hestercombe, Taunton

212   Mughal Garden, Lister Park, Bradford

216   Carpet Garden, Highgrove, Tetbury

222   Acknowledgements

Hestercombe, Taunton

Carpet Garden, Highgrove, Tetbury

Mughal Garden, Lister Park, Bradford

ENGLAND

Topkapi Palace, Istanbul
Emirgan Park, Istanbul

Real Alcázar, Seville

Urquijo Garden (Palacio de Galiana), Toledo

SPAIN

The Alhambra, Granada

TURKEY

MOROCCO

Umberto Pasti Garden, Tangier

The Chellah, Rabat

Agdal, Marrakech
Palais Lamrani Riad, Marrakech
Le Jardin Secret, Marrakech
Le Jardin Majorelle, Marrakech

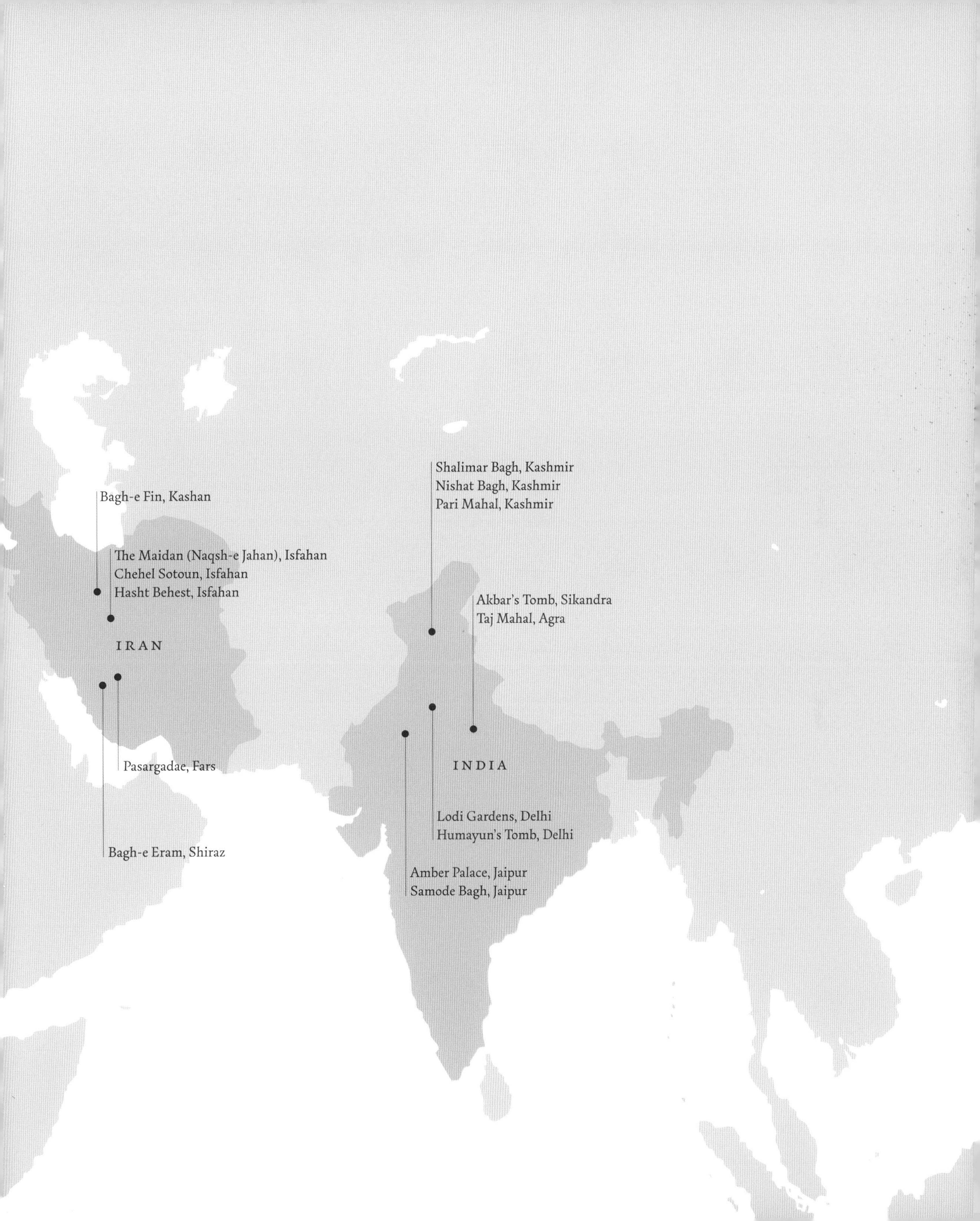

Bagh-e Fin, Kashan

Shalimar Bagh, Kashmir
Nishat Bagh, Kashmir
Pari Mahal, Kashmir

The Maidan (Naqsh-e Jahan), Isfahan
Chehel Sotoun, Isfahan
Hasht Behest, Isfahan

Akbar's Tomb, Sikandra
Taj Mahal, Agra

I R A N

I N D I A

Pasargadae, Fars

Lodi Gardens, Delhi
Humayun's Tomb, Delhi

Bagh-e Eram, Shiraz

Amber Palace, Jaipur
Samode Bagh, Jaipur

Introduction

The Arabian desert is remorseless. Fly over it and the barren vastness is daunting, but to spend your life moving through it on foot, on the edge of survival, is beyond imagination. The only thing that makes life possible, let alone bearable, is an oasis. Without occasional patches of green with fresh water, there would be no life at all. Compared to the intolerable heat, the sandstorms, the interminable salt flats and the razor-sharp rocks, an oasis is heaven on earth.

The nomadic desert Arabs lived in the harshest and least fertile of environments that could support any kind of human life. By the time of the prophet Muhammad in the early seventh century AD, a garden was something they arrived at as more than just a relief from the rigours of the desert but a symbol of life underlined by the one great essential – water.

It is a common cliché to refer to your garden as 'a little bit of heaven' or as 'paradise'. This is shorthand for saying that it seems just about perfect, combining beauty and peace and – momentarily at least – it is devoid of all care. But for the desert Arabs of the sixth and seventh centuries, an oasis really was paradise and paradise was inevitably going to be just like the perfect oasis, running with water, full of fruits and green with luxuriant shade.

The Koran made all this explicit. There are over 120 references to the gardens of paradise, and the phrase most often mentioned is 'gardens underneath which rivers flow'. Water in physical form flowing through and beneath gardens and flowing within this beautiful, abundant peaceful place is the heart and essence of the paradise garden.

The concept of paradise being a garden goes back almost five thousand years to Babylon, but the first reference to the word comes from the Persian *pairidaeza* which means an enclosed garden filled with trees – and especially fruit trees. This pre-dates the Islamic idea of a paradise garden by at least a thousand years. By 530 BC Cyrus the Great had made a large garden at his palace at Pasargadae complete with sophisticated water channels and pools.

When the Arabs conquered Persia in 650 they took on the idea of the four-part *charhar bagh*. This became the model for paradise gardens throughout the Islamic world thereafter, albeit with many variations. The four rivers, of milk, honey, water and wine flow from its centre. Four is a magic and holy number and the cube the perfect shape, so four features in every paradise garden and the number eight, derived from it, is also very common. The central fountain with flowing water is also essential. Moving water is the key for many

reasons. The movement symbolises life, but it has great practical implications too. Water cools and dampens the air, it produces a musical sound that is conducive to contemplation and peace and it can be used for irrigation.

All fruits were grown – often in deeply sunken beds so the tops of the trees were at head height for those standing on the paths dividing the charhar bagh – although rarely in mixed orchards. Olive and fig, date and pomegranate were ubiquitous and symbolically important. The orange arrived from India via the Silk Road by the eleventh century, and was planted throughout gardens primarily for the fragrance and beauty of its flowers and fruit but also as a bitter oil in cooking; the sweet orange came much later. Flowers would be grown beneath the fruit trees but not in borders as such. In any event flowering was largely restricted to a brief spring explosion before the searing heat kicked in.

It is hard for northern Europeans to imagine the extreme summer heat of the desert or places such as northern India where the temperature can rise above 50 degrees. Shade, coolness and green repose become the greatest luxuries. Fragrance, gentle sound, good company, beautiful carpets and silks and delicious fruits are a sensual refinement. Add to all this the sense of safety and harmony that come within the protective confines of a domestic garden, and you have a good measure of paradise – and the knowledge that this is just a cloudy reflection of true paradise, merely an inkling of the heaven that awaits.

Derry Moore and I set out to visit the paradise gardens featured in this book as much to learn about them as anything else. Although they all are shaped and informed by Islam, they cover such a wide range of locations and cultures – from Spain through Iran and across to Agra in India – that they reveal a variety and sophistication that matches any other kind of garden. Some I had visited before, and many I had read about. A few were completely new to me. But seeing them all in the space of a few months, across such a range of countries and situations, was not just hugely enjoyable but has also expanded my gardening knowledge and awareness in a way that no other series of gardens has done before. These glimpses into paradise have certainly made me a better gardener, and perhaps a better person.

ABOVE
The gardens at the Real
Alcázar in Seville have
evolved to combine the best
of Moorish and Spanish
influences to create a
unique style of garden,
preserving the best of both
cultures.

OPPOSITE
Light spangles through
a jaali of ornate marble
lattice inside Humayun's
tomb in Delhi.

IRAN

THE CALL CAME THROUGH AT THE END OF A LONG DAY FILMING
in my own garden.

'A press visa has come through for you and Derry to go to Iran for five days.' 'When?'
'In three days' time. Do you still want to go?'

Did I want to go? I had wanted to go to see the gardens of Iran for most of my adult
life . . . Getting a tourist visa to visit gardens in Iran is straightforward enough, but a press
one is a whole different matter. This visa arrived after over six months of application and
lobbying, and after all hope of success had been abandoned.

Any attempt to understand or appreciate the gardens of Islam has to go via Iran.
The very word paradise comes directly from the Old Persian word *pairidaeza* which means a
walled garden. Persian kings were expected to excel in the art of gardening as much as that
of war, and Cyrus the Great's garden at Pasargadae, dating back to the sixth century BC,
was not an invention but, rather, a fine example of an existing part of Persian civilisation.
Certainly by the first century BC, the Romans who invaded Persia were captivated by the
gardens and began to imitate them back in Rome.

Of course Cyrus's garden was not Islamic, and the Zoroastrian religion was not
replaced until a thousand years later, after the Arab invasion in the seventh century AD.

OPPOSITE
*The Imam Mosque in the
Maidan square is one of
the world's great buildings
whose huge volumes of
sifted light are matched
by the complexity of the
decorative tilework.*

RIGHT
*Water is the key to all
paradise gardens – not
least because it cools the
intense heat of summer.*

The huge cypresses of Bagh-e Fin were planted when Shah Abbas remade the garden at the beginning of the seventeenth century. Each one is now accompanied by a sapling growing in its lea so, when its inevitable time comes, the replacement will be established.

But if the Arabs brought Islam to Persia, they took the paradise garden as their own. In fact they brought little other than their calligraphy and creed, and absorbed the cultures they conquered with ease and great tolerance. Certainly the pairidaezas seemed earthly manifestations of the Koranic paradise, with their ordered representation of life based around water and the privacy of a walled garden. So these Persian gardens provided the framework for all future paradise gardens created in the Arab world, from Syria down through Egypt, Sicily and Spain.

As well as the nature of the pairidaezas, with their enclosed charhar baghs and symbolic fruit trees, the Persian gardens were not solely utilitarian. They inextricably combined poetry and a love of flowers with gardens, and the ideal – represented in countless miniatures – was to recline on carpets woven from the finest wool or silk, in the shade of a pavilion, tent or fruit tree, surrounded by the fragrance of roses, listening to poetry, the song of the nightingale and gently rippling water.

Persian gardens were, therefore, sensuous, romantic places rather than just symbols of life contrasted with the harshness of the desert. Any lover of gardens sooner or later discovers these wonderful, almost mythical places and longs to see them. If that person is also attempting to understand and discover as much as possible about Islamic gardens in general, then the draw is irresistible. Which is why I was more than happy to drop everything and set off with barely more than a couple of phone numbers, a list of gardens and just four days in which to see them. Crazily inadequate, but absolutely essential.

So, Derry and I found ourselves sitting in a deserted Isfahan airport at three in the morning while a growing group of deeply suspicious officials scrutinised our passports. 'Gardens,' they kept saying, 'what gardens? Why? Who for?' For about an hour it seemed that we were, at best, likely to be sent on the next plane back to Istanbul. But, once they were convinced we were not up to any mischief, there followed four days of superb hospitality, fascinating gardens and stunning scenery. The surface was only scratched but it set up an itch to return as soon as they will have me back.

Pasargadae

FARS

We rose long before dawn to travel into the desert blackness from Isfahan to Fars, the rising sun revealing a stony desert flanked on either horizon by grey mountains as stark as elephant hide. After three hours we stopped to have breakfast by the side of the road with eggs brought down the street hot in their pans, great discs of flatbread and salty cheese from a goatskin bag.

Another couple of hours on the road brought us to Pasargadae on the Plain of Murghab, the site of the palace of Cyrus the Great, built where he defeated the Medes in 550 BC. There is little to see today except one incongruously huge pillar standing alone, a few other sections marking a pavilion and a fort, made out of huge blocks of stone, which is being excavated by a team in wellingtons and headscarves. The sun burns down but the plain is fertile and has been cultivated for the last 5,000 years. In the distance, a swathe of green is being grazed by a large flock of goats whose neck bells jangle tinnily. But this empty plain holds one particular treasure over a kilometre long. This is a stone-lined channel about a foot wide marking out a quartered garden, interspersed every 40 feet or so with basins, each cut from a single stone block about 3 feet square. This channel, fully 3 feet below the modern surface of the plain, is in the process of being patiently restored, using the fragments of stone in the ground and revetted with banks of sieved earth from the archaeology mixed with water and straw. The result is a broad canal with beautifully smooth plaster banks and a stone rill running along its base. Set in the almost featureless plain, it becomes a hypnotic piece of land art.

The division of the garden into four quarters sets the model for the traditional charhar bagh that is still used today. However, the divisions were not Islamic, but represented the Zoroastrian elements of fire, air, earth and water.

As for the plants of Cyrus's garden, future investigations may find evidence of seeds and plant material, but tulips and irises would have been underplanted beneath trees, including the cypress and plane for shade, but which would otherwise have been dominated by fruit including the sour cherry, not least for its elegant spring blossom. The even earlier flowering almond and native pomegranate would have grown as enthusiastically then as now, but the orange, so prevalent in later paradise gardens, did not reach Persia for about another 1,500 years.

❦

OPPOSITE ABOVE
The tomb of Cyrus the Great, made at his death in 530 BC, still dominates the plain of Pasargadae. Inside the tomb is this inscription: 'O man, I am Cyrus who acquired the empire for the Persians and was king of Asia; grudge me not, therefore, my monument.'

OPPOSITE BELOW
The stone-lined water-courses that mark out Cyrus's garden were interspersed with regular square basins every 30 feet or so, each one cut from a single block of limestone.

OVERLEAF
Cyrus's palace at Pasargadae was set on the great open Plain of Murghab where he won his most famous battle against the Medes. The palace was huge and splendid although all that now remains above ground are the stubs of a few huge pillars.

Bagh-e Fin

KASHAN

Kashan is famously a city of silks, carpets, ceramics and rose water distilled from native damask roses. However, when we arrived at midnight after a three-hour drive in the bumpy dark, the roads were clogged with drivers all trying to hoot their horns as often as possible, silks and rose water seemed rather distant. Next morning, I rose at four to drive for a few hours across the salt flats to see the sun rise in the desert, eating breakfast of flatbread, olives and local cheese spread on a carpet on the sand. Romanticism had returned.

And romanticism remained because the purpose of the trip to Kashan was to visit Bagh-e Fin, acknowledged as one of Iran's great gardens and the oldest one extant. There was a walled garden on the site by the beginning of the sixteenth century but most of what we see now dates from 1590 and is the work of the greatest Safavid ruler Shah Abbas I, who established a series of caravanserais along the route from Isfahan to the Caspian Sea where he could conduct government business, hunt and make the journey for himself and his court more pleasurable.

As you enter the great gate through the high walls, you are met with a narrow rill studded with bubbling fountains. Paths flanked by huge cypresses – many from the original early seventeenth-century planting – follow its course to a pavilion built at the beginning of the nineteenth century. Turquoise faience tiles run like a kingfisher flash of electric colour under all the rills, cascades and pools.

Of all the gardens in Iran, this is the one where the sheer delight in water was most obvious. At every turn children played in it, visitors dabbled their hands or walked barefoot through it. Every photograph involved some watery element as a backdrop. This is water as a celebration rather than a display. Water as life.

Before I visited Bagh-e Fin, I was warned that the garden was a pale shadow of its former self and had been allowed to fall into ruin over the past twenty years or so. Undoubtedly it would be both more authentic and more beautiful if the many symmetrical beds made by the intersecting paths and water channels were filled with fruit trees, roses and spring bulbs rather than bare soil and patchy grass. But that is easy to fix. Its magical essence remains intact, palpable and untouched by time.

꽃

OPPOSITE
Water is literally at the heart of the garden at Bagh-e-Fin, rising into a square basin at the centre of the pavilion before flowing out into the garden.

OPPOSITE
A family group, with the studiousness of the pose diminishing as the age ascends!

RIGHT ABOVE & BELOW
Turquoise faience tiles line all the rills and pools with a kingfisher flash of electric colour. These were made locally and many in the garden are original, dating back over 400 years.

OVERLEAF
The central, square pavilion at Bagh-e-Fin was built in the early nineteenth century to replace an earlier building damaged by an earthquake.

ABOVE
Four circular towers are set in the curtain wall to protect the garden both from potential enemies and the desert landscape around, creating the pairidaeza or walled garden.

All the water in this parched desert site comes via the system of qanats. These were underground tunnels taking water from the melting snows of the mountains down to the plains and delivering it along the way, as needed, by means of shafts sunk into the tunnels which gravity would then fill for irrigation without halting the flow further down the line. At Bagh-e Fin there is a huge water cistern above the garden and each visible canal has a channel beneath it which, when blocked, forces water up through the many fountains that stud all the rills.

A restaurant in Kashan.
Guests – often whole
families or groups of
friends – sit cross-legged
on these divans and meals
are served spread out on
the carpeted base, with
everyone sharing dishes
invariably eaten with
spoons and pieces torn from
great discs of flatbread.
It is a supremely civilised
way to enjoy delicious food.

The Maidan (Naqsh-e Jahan)

ISFAHAN

The Maidan – or Naqsh-e Jahan Square – is physically, religiously, commercially and horticulturally the centre of Isfahan. It is enormous: over 8 hectares in area, 500 metres long by 170 wide, it is seven times the size of St Mark's Square, Venice, and was built when Shah Abbas II moved the capital of the Safavid dynasty to Isfahan at the beginning of the seventeenth century. He converted what had been an irregular marketplace into this formal rectangle with monumental buildings on each side.

On the west was the Ali Qapu (Sublime Portal) pavilion where ambassadors were lodged and where the shah could sit and look down on his people from a verandah supported by huge wooden pillars and, as importantly, be seen by them. Remote, on high, but always present. Opposite Ali Qapu is the private mosque of Sheikh Lotfollah, named after the father of one of Shah Abbas's wives, intended originally for the shah's harem. The exterior of the mosque is completely covered with a dazzling intensity of blue floral tiles, but the interior light, filtered into filigreed spangles through high, latticed windows below the dome, takes that flamboyance and makes it sublime. The azure blue is balanced by ochres and gold and turquoise ribbing, the tiles decorated with floral designs and calligraphic inscriptions. Stepping into that arching space is a breathtaking experience. At the south end of the square is the much bigger public Imam Mosque with its famous turquoise towers and huge internal volumes filled with an enormity of light and shade. Finally, at the opposite end of the square was the grand entrance to the Imperial Bazaar that specialised in carpets.

Arcading the entire square are shops and workshops, largely unchanged since their inception 500 years ago when Shah Abbas effectively re-routed the Silk Road to pass through the city, encouraging visitors, trade and diplomatic contact with Europe and the West. The Maidan itself was originally used for polo, parades and public punishments, and a broad canal ran right round the outside which is now a road used only by ranks of horse-drawn tourist carriages. But tourists are in a minority, and as the afternoon light thins the enormous space becomes busy with activity. Scores of families, dominated by women in black chadors, spread carpets on both the grass and paving, unpack picnics, light stoves for tea and share their evening meal while around them men stroll and talk, and lovers meet. It is a scene that cannot have changed much since the days of Shah Abbas.

❦

The square was originally
used as a polo pitch.
The only traffic allowed
is the horse-drawn
carriages queuing up to
trot tourists gently around
the perimeter, along a road
that was once a canal that
ran between the pitch and
the arcaded shops and
workshops that still run
around the outside, almost
unchanged since they were
built in the early
seventeenth century.

ABOVE
Quinces grow especially
well in Iran and are used
in many savoury dishes.

Drinking water in the grounds of the garden shaded from the sun with bespoke pavilions, both for coolness and privacy.

Hasht Behest

ISFAHAN

Originally the charhar bagh avenue had dozens of palaces and gardens lining its route, but now only two remain, Chehel Sotoun and Hasht Behest or 'Eight Paradises'. The name refers to the pavilion at its centre, built in 1669 and originally set within a much larger Garden of the Nightingale. The eight paradises are set in brick and stone and, like the name Hasht Behest, this was not an uncommon architectural device. The octagonal building consists of two floors with an octagonal room in each corner, giving a total of eight rooms. The arrangement of four rooms on each floor relates to the quadrants of the charhar bagh and its common division into eight terraces or parterres, so the structures of the garden and the building are connected both visually and symbolically.

The result is open and feels tent-like rather than a grand palace. An octagonal pool sits beneath a domed vault in the middle of the ground floor with a central jet, the water spilling beneath the floor into basins and then emerging outside down cascades into a waterway that runs right round the pavilion. High arches frame the garden and the long central basin with its arching fountains cools the air.

Unlike Chehel Sotoun, where you take your selfie with the columns reflected in the water and then troop out. Hasht Behest is a public park and I have never been anywhere that seemed to be so enjoyed – so well utilised – as opposed to merely visited. Dozens of groups were picnicking on striped carpets, both on the grass under the trees and, seemingly just as comfortably, on the paved paths. This love of sitting and eating in groups outdoors seems to be wired into daily Iranian life just as it has been since the time of Cyrus the Great. It is more than just flopping down on a patch of grass to chat, but a stately and ritualistic process. A carpet is put down, tea is made, food and conversation are shared, all in the green shade of a garden.

The garden is made noble by its long walks lined with huge cypresses, planes and elms, although the latter have become old and much pruned. The trees almost touch to become a 100-foot-high hedge. White roses line the paths. It is a green, full-grown place, luxuriant with shade and made colourful and beautiful by people rather than plants.

OPPOSITE

Few gardens can give so much communal pleasure as the grounds of Hasht Behest.

OVERLEAF

While hijab is mandatory in Iran it takes many forms, from a simple headscarf to – as here – the full chador.

RIGHT

One of the unique features of all Iranian public gardens is the way that families and groups of friends share meals and drink tea, made on a stove, sitting on a carpet. This might be on the grass or equally the paving. Then, when they are ready to go, the food will be carefully packed away into enormous bags and the carpet scrupulously swept clean, rolled up and the group will drift slowly away to their homes.

Bagh-e Eram

Bagh-e Eram, the 'Garden of Heaven', is in the centre of Shiraz, the city of roses, nightingales, poetry and wine. It has ancient roots but a more actively modern present than any of the other gardens I visited in Iran. Although it is the site of a garden begun in the twelfth century, it was both planted and the pavilion built in the nineteenth century, so the cypresses and pines are now mature and stately.

The pavilion has a rakish charm that is quite different from the Safavid buildings in Isfahan or Kashan, and is fronted by a large square basin with turquoise water that feeds a water system that travels down various levels via stepped cascades, along the centre of paths, around the edge of avenues of clipped oranges and laurels and on along a rill out beyond the garden's edge. There is real grandeur and sweep to this.

Since 1983 the garden has been part of Shiraz Botanical Garden, so the planting is far more varied and intense than most other Iranian gardens, adding colour and texture and more botanical interest. There is a large collection of roses, grown in rows divided by grass paths looking altogether more botanical than garden, but the emphasis on flowers comes as a pleasant change from the general absence of them elsewhere. To achieve this floral effect relies upon plants from all over the world rather than purely native species, because although Persian gardens would be filled with flowers in the spring, flowers would be very thin on the ground in summer without the introduction of plants from around the world.

Like Hasht Behest, Bagh-e Eram was filled with families and students walking, sitting in groups and picnicking, clearly relishing every aspect of the garden, and this full and daily use of the garden is something integral to the life of the city.

Although there is a wide mix of plants from the West in the borders nearest the pavilion, the deeply sunken beds of the charhar bargh contain orchards of pomegranates and bitter oranges – never mixed – in an entirely authentic manner, their branches and fruits at easy plucking height as one saunters down the broad paved paths between them, and I was assured that when the orange blossom is in flower in April the whole city is filled with its fragrance, which is why Shiraz is called 'the paradise of Iran'.

❦

OPPOSITE
The chador-clad women make stark silhouettes against the intensely ornate surfaces of the Bagh-e-Eram pavilion.

OVERLEAF
The pavilion was built in the middle of the nineteenth century and faces south on to a large square basin.

ABOVE
The fronds of a date palm
– essential to all paradise
gardens – mirror the spray
and fall of the fountain.

OPPOSITE
The garden is open to the
public and much used as
a place where local people
can meet and relax.

*Bagh-e Eram is now
part of Shiraz Botanical
Garden and is a World
Heritage Site. Although
this means that it has
a much wider range of
plants than most paradise
gardens, these clipped
orange trees still represent
the formality and
symmetry that remains
at its heart.*

INDIA

INDIA TAKES NO PRISONERS. NO OTHER COUNTRY IS SO EXHAUSTING, exhilarating, demanding, fulfilling or full of life in all its best and worst excesses. The colours seem to be brighter, the heat hotter, the noise louder and the traffic more chaotic (if inexhaustibly good-tempered) than can be imagined in most other parts of the world, let alone emulated.

All this is at odds with the world of calm, contemplative seclusion that shapes both the actuality of most paradise gardens and the idea behind all of them. Yet India is the home of the Mughals and the Mughals are an essential part of the story of these gardens.

The Mughals did not bring Islam to India – that had preceded them by 500 years with Islamic invaders from the north and west, before Genghis Khan and then Timur ravaged through northern India in the thirteenth and fourteenth centuries respectively. But what the first Mughal ruler, Babur, brought when he came down from Kabul with his army in 1526 was a love of gardens. Despite a reverence for nature, neither the Muslim Delhi sultanate nor the Hindu Rajput dynasties made gardens and, despite seeing great significance and symbolism in landscape, they did not seek to impose symmetry or order on to nature in the way that the Persian culture had been doing for the previous 2,000 years.

OPPOSITE
The Taj Mahal seen across the lawns put in by the British viceroy Lord Curzon at the beginning of the twentieth century. Lovely, but historically completely inaccurate.

RIGHT
A chadar in Nishat Bagh, Kashmir, where the abundant supply of water entranced the Mughals.

OPPOSITE
The lobby of Akbar's tomb is like being inside the core of a gemstone.

Babur was born in 1483 near Samarkand in modern Uzbekistan and established his kingdom around Kabul. He was descended from both Genghis Khan and Timur but despite being a great warrior, he spoke two languages, was a poet and a musician and created gardens wherever he went. It is said that he preferred tents to buildings and often conducted his affairs from a tented canopy in one of his gardens. In Humayun's tomb gardens in Delhi you can see the raised platforms where paths meet, now often planted with a single tree but almost certainly intended for these tents under which carpets would be spread and courtly life lived outside.

Although the Mughals were not Persian, the folk memory of Persia was an important influence on them. Persian was used as the main language at court and the Persian charhar bagh was the model for all their gardens with its four divisions, flowing water and sunken beds planted with fruits. The buildings around which these gardens were based were the perfect – in many cases sublime – combination of Islamic architecture and building techniques and Indo craftsmanship, especially stone carving. One of the myths still prevalent about the Taj Mahal is that the craftsmen were brought in from Italy – as if only Europeans had the necessary skills. Nothing could be further from the truth and the same skills – often in the same families – are still evident today, though arguably they reached their pinnacle in the great Mughal period of 1550 to 1650.

While these buildings are often beautifully maintained and restored, the gardens in which they are centred are usually less well tended or understood. It would be a great act of cultural enlightenment if, say, the charbaghs of the Taj Mahal or Humayan's tomb were to be restored to their original planting and glory with the same scholarship, and we could see these great paradise gardens in all their sublime glory.

Sari-clad women collect
flowers of the chandni tree
in the early morning to
make into garlands in the
courtyard at the Amber
Palace, outside Jaipur.

Lodi Gardens

DELHI

When Babur swept down into northern India from Kabul, his final conquest was the defeat of the Lodi Emperor Ibrahim in 1526 at the Battle of Panipat, thus ending seventy-five years of Lodi rule. Like Babur, the Lodis were Sunni Muslims who had built tombs grouped in what was considered an auspicious spot in Delhi, now known as Lodi Gardens. They contain the best surviving Lodi architectural remains as well as the extremely rare extant Sayyid building with the tomb of Muhammed Shah, the last Sayyid ruler.

The gardens today are not in any sense paradise gardens but are a link to the successive rule of Sayyids, Lodis, Mughals and the British. The very British landscaped lake was actually the original water supply from the Yamuna River for Sikander Lodi's tomb and it is crossed by a Mughal bridge, the Athpular, built during Akbar's reign. The planting around it is post-1930s British.

More significantly, there is no record of organised gardens around these Lodi tombs. In fact villages grew up around them quite soon after the Mughal conquest, and it was not until the 1930s that they were cleared and a garden was made on the site. This was overseen by Lady Willingdon, wife of the Governor General Lord Willingdon who imprisoned Gandhi and 80,000 activists and, when he retired from the viceroyship in 1936, was the last man to be made a marquess. Lady Willingdon's Park – as it was known until independence – with its ninety acres of mature trees, open grassy spaces, ponds and topiary is free to anyone and open to all every day from dawn to dusk, and has remained as a much-loved and much-used green lung in an increasingly smog-enveloped, traffic-choked Delhi. The result is more like a subtropical Stourhead or Stowe than a paradise garden, the huge ruins acting as eye-catchers or strategically placed points of interest rather than the focus of the gardens around them.

Beneath the great dome of the Bara Gumbad the light is reduced to the high window arches, and excited children run in and out with none of the hushed reverence that the Mughal tombs inspire. Outside a hundred schoolgirls in identical uniforms are having a dance class. A dozen large eagles strut on the grass like matadors. Six gardeners frantically clip the topiary with heavy hand shears and joggers solemnly complete their laps, lost in the world of their headphones.

❦

OPPOSITE
The tomb of Muhammed Shah, the last Sayyid ruler who died in 1445. It is one of the very few surviving Sayyid buildings from the pre-Lodi era.

OPPOSITE
The Shish Gumbad or 'Glass Dome' is a muscular, square building made from great blocks of quartz beneath a large dome. The dome was originally faced with blue enamelled tiles which gave it its name.

RIGHT ABOVE
The pre-Mughal mosque set to one side of the Bara Gumbad.

BELOW
Date palms set up an abstract yet regular rhythm of clean trunks.

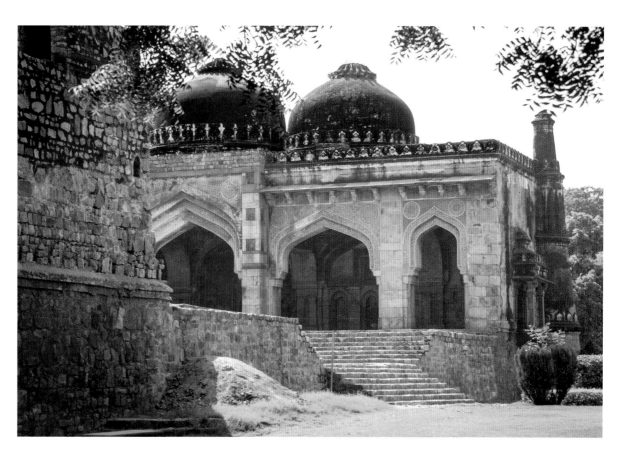

ABOVE

The buildings of the Lodi Gardens occupy the park in an unlikely combination of the walls of a burnt-down mansion and the structures of an eighteenth-century British landscape park.

Looking through from the Shish Gumbad to the mosque outside the Bara Gumbad. These surviving Lodi buildings have none of the elaborate decoration or finesse of the later Mughal tombs, yet their robustness and solidity that have survived half a millennium add great character to the gardens.

Humayun's Tomb

DELHI

To walk into Humayun's tomb at dawn and see the sun slip up over the shoulder of the great rose and silver building, made sunset orange by the Delhi smog, is one of the great gardening experiences of any life.

The creation of large walled charbaghs around the tombs of rulers and generals is the most significant innovation that the Mughals brought to garden design. (The Mughals, who largely spoke Persian at court, made the charbaghs very similar to the Persian charhar baghs.) The tomb gardens are invariably on a single level and hark back to Persian gardens rather than the Mughal gardens of Kashmir that use the slopes and terraces both for the movement of water and the elevated views.

The level ground centred around a great building gives the tomb gardens immense gravitas and calm. Yet they were not solemn places to walk in with reverential hush. The modern visitor shares the gardens with yoga classes and retired army officers in their tracksuits and swagger sticks striding and chatting as they take their morning constitutional which then elides into a series of yoga exercises that defy the pot bellies and thickened necks. From the outset, as now, it seems the gardens were used for pleasure, work and sensual enjoyment. With the combination of the beautiful monument to the dead set in this vibrantly living charbagh, the idealised paradise garden was created.

Humayun was the feckless son of the great Babur. A sensualist, weak and deeply superstitious – it is said that he would never enter a room left foot first – he was not equal to the task of securing the kingdom that Babur had conquered, and was slowly driven back to Persia by a succession of defeats by Indian princes. Having eventually reconquered Kabul and Kandahar from his brothers, he did not return to Delhi to take up his crown until July 1555. But within six months he heard the call to prayer, turned to descend the steep stairs of his library, tripped on his gown and tumbled to his death. The staircase up into his tomb is said to be extra steep to commemorate that fall.

The tomb was built by his wife Haji Begam between 1563 and 1572, and was designed by a Persian architect from Herat who used the Timurid double-skinned dome – the first of what became the most distinctive Mughal contribution to Indian architecture.
❦

OPPOSITE
Looking through the entrance gateway down towards Humayun's tomb with the rill seemingly running under and through the great mausoleum.

OVERLEAF
Humayun's tomb is set on a level platform that runs right round the building, and the original planting in the sunken beds would not have been allowed to grow any taller than the platform to ensure that the view of the building was not obscured.

OPPOSITE
In the dawn light the red sandstone glows in every shade of peachy pink.

RIGHT ABOVE
The raised platforms at the intersections of paths would originally have been spread with carpets and then set with canopies and tents as places for discussion, poetry and music.

BELOW
Although they are beautiful and provide delicious shade, the size of the modern trees far exceeds anything that was intended in the original planting.

ABOVE

Only the lower end of the garden has retained the original depth of the sunken beds, with those around the mausoleum filled in practically to path level. The path around the edge of the sunken area *would originally have been planted so the tops of the trees were head height to passers-by on the elevated walkways.*

OPPOSITE

Water, dissecting the path like a blade, is the key to the garden. While much else remains unrestored, all the rills, basins and waterways are carefully preserved.

Amber Palace

JAIPUR

Amber had existed as a fortress since the tenth century but it was enlarged and made into the palace by the Hindu Raja Man Singh who completed it in 1600. This coincides with the rules of Shah Abbas in Persia, Suleyman the Magnificent in Istanbul and Akbar in Agra.

In the heart of the palace, up through the Ganesh Gate, is the private garden, directly outside and below the Sukh Mandir. This Islamic charbagh with its white marble floors and plastered walls was exclusively for the royal family's summer occupation. Fed by a tank on the roof, the back wall had a cascade that passed over a perforated marble screen so the breeze could flow through and be cooled by the water which ran into a basin in the floor and along a channel, down the scalloped pigeon-breast surface of a chadar and on into the garden. The whole effect of the water would have been lively, cooling and musical.

The Hindu Rajputs practised cremation rather than burial so did not construct tombs. Although Hinduism holds the belief in reincarnation and the continuation of life, there is no afterlife or concept of paradise per se, therefore the charbagh becomes a contemporary design trope rather than having a profound meaning, as it did for Muslims. Nevertheless, the integration and hybridisation of the Muslim and Hindu courts was noticeable and contributed much to the success of the Mughal invasion. By allowing Hindus to practise their religion and to govern their own lands and people, they gained loyalty and avoided expensive and potentially disastrous wars.

Raja Man Singh of Amber had been raised in the Mughal court and was one of Akbar's trusted generals. Akbar married one of his daughters and Amber became a symbol of the integration between the two courts, cultures and religions. In that context the charbagh at Amber can be seen as a political statement of loyalty as much as anything else.

The Saffron Garden, or Kesar Kyari, was supposedly planted with saffron so the ladies of the harem could look down on it and smell the fragrance from the thousands of little mauve flowers far below. It is a good story but the garden was probably never made and, if it was, it certainly did not last because Rajasthan is much too hot and dry for saffron crocus to thrive.

❦

OPPOSITE
Looking across the lake from the eighteenth-century Dil-Aaram Bagh to the chadar running from the much earlier saffron garden at Amber.

OVERLEAF
Looking down from the harem at the top of the palace to Kesar Kyari, or the saffron garden, with its Mughal-influenced charbagh in this Hindu Rajput palace. This was a garden always intended to be viewed from above as part of the dramatic panorama below and beyond the palace walls.

The private Mughal garden was solely for the use of the royal family and is directly outside their summer quarters. The charbagh lies in a sunken square below with blocks of green intercut with marble paving so narrow that it is clearly not for walking, but solely for access. In the centre of the charbagh are fountains from a star-shaped pool. The clipped green is in a series of triangles making hexagons and lozenges which are Hindu rather than Muslim shapes. But the whole existence and manifestation of the charbagh at Amber is a curious but ultimately incredibly successful intermarriage of cultures.

Diwan-i-Am, the 'Hall of Public Audience', was built at the same time as the Taj Mahal, between 1630 and 1640, at the height of the Mughal power and influence.

Akbar's Tomb

SIKANDRA

Akbar was only thirteen when his father Humayun died, but by the time of his death in 1605 he was the much-loved ruler of a vast and expanding empire, and he is now recognised as one of the great Mughal rulers. Although he was unable to read or write, he was learned and encouraged beautiful buildings and gardens. He also developed a new religion – based upon himself as a divine centre of faith – that was tolerant and embraced all faiths.

Immediately after Akbar's death, his son Jahangir began Akbar's tomb garden at Sikandra, just outside Agra – Akbar's capital, where he died. It is huge, set in a vast charbagh called Behishtabad, 'Abode of Paradise', and in every way more ornate than that of Humayun. The Mughals had become grander, hence their monuments were grander too. It uses the same lovely peach-coloured sandstone, but as you approach the entrance gate you cannot fail to notice that the white marble inlay is much more ornate and the walls more densely covered with Persian inscriptions. Minarets rise in all four corners like, as has been unkindly pointed out, a very ornate Battersea Power Station.

The tomb itself does not have the Timurid dome of Humayun's mausoleum but instead a cluster of Hindu *chhatris*, indicating the assimilation of Mughal and local architecture and culture. It is approached by a path a full 25 yards wide like a great paved town square that is set high above four equal sections of the charbagh, now fringed with palms, and the cropped lawns laid out with British landscaping and grazed by deer, peacocks and squabbling macaques. There are water channels down each of the paths, meeting in large square pools at the midpoint – I would love to see them flowing with water but on both occasions I have visited in the last ten years they have been bone dry.

Inside the mausoleum is one of the most intensely decorated, resplendent chambers on earth: russets and ochres picked out with lapis, silver and gold flowers and swirling calligraphy. But Akbar's actual tomb, down a dark ramp, is an empty, unadorned vault, the small square light of the door facing towards Mecca at the centre of this huge building surrounded by the vast paradise garden filled with fruits and flowers which, in turn, was at the heart of one of the largest kingdoms the world has ever known.

OPPOSITE
A dry pool, once filled by the rill leading to it, stands in front of a portal leading east to a pavilion and gate at the edge of the charbagh. Without water these gardens become rooms.

OVERLEAF
Akbar was one of the greatest Mughal leaders and his tomb is altogether more ornate than that of his father Humayun. The tomb takes the form of a tiered pyramid with the upper storeys built as pillared kiosks in a mixture of Islamic and Hindu styles.

ABOVE
The charbagh has many
mature trees that cast
a deliciously cool green
shade.

OPPOSITE
In the archways around
the perimeter of the tomb
the pastel tones and shapes
echo as they recede.

Taj Mahal

AGRA

It is said that you should never meet your heroes. Certainly the Taj Mahal staggers under the weight of expectation of every visitor, yet it seems to surpass the wildest hope. It really is one of the great creative miracles that mankind has risen to.

Whereas the tomb gardens of Humayun and Akbar are monuments to kingship, erected posthumously as much to preserve their worldly honour as for their eternal souls, the Taj Mahal is simply and gloriously a monument to boundless love. Mumtaz, the favourite wife of Shah Jahan, grandson of Akbar and ruler of the Mughal kingdom (1627–57) died in 1631 giving birth to their fourteenth child, and the Taj, set in gardens on both sides of the river, is her tomb. Shah Jahan was laid by her side when he died twenty-six years after her. The facts that he presided over one of the most lavish courts that the world has ever seen and had untold riches and power with which to express the scale of his love, do not reduce its essence. It is a story that every heart understands.

Work began in 1632 and it took twelve years and 25,000 craftsmen to complete the tomb itself, with another ten years required to finish the entire paradise garden complex with mosque, pavilions and gateways. The statistics reel off as though there is need for superhuman effort to explain something that appears so artlessly beautiful. While the marble tomb, silvery in the dawn light (it was known by the Mughals as the 'luminous' tomb) inevitably draws every eye, this is a tomb garden with a charbagh in four quarters between the gatehouse and mausoleum, and a huge central raised pool where the bisecting paths meet. Each quadrant of the charbagh is subdivided into four and all the paths are of pale red sandstone which casts a pink glow on the marble building, making it light and feminine as opposed to the muscular authority of other tomb gardens.

The planting of the original garden has gone, replaced by well-meaning but wholly inaccurate British lawns and trees. Perhaps every culture unwittingly remakes its own version of heaven, and for the British in India that meant lawns and tall trees. But Shah Jahan would surely have known these beds when they were many feet deeper and filled with the fruit and fragrance of a Koranic paradise.

❦

OPPOSITE
The silver marble of the tomb reflects the sky, and as the sun rises through the soupy dawn smog, the building glows pink.

OVERLEAF
The Mehtab Bagh, or 'Moonlight Garden', was discovered twenty-five years ago on the other side of the Yamuna River. This doubles the size of the garden and places the tomb in the middle – like other tomb gardens – rather than at one end. Its use was reserved exclusively for the shah and was intended as the ideal place to see the Taj by moonlight.

ABOVE

Over the centuries the Yamuna River in Agra has become silted and has shifted slightly, but originally it lapped the walls of the Taj and the many other gardens that lined its banks.

OPPOSITE

A rare shot of an empty corner of the garden. As many as 70,000 visitors a day come to see the Taj, with a total of over 6.5 million a year.

Shalimar Bagh

KASHMIR

The Mughals loved Kashmir. Its coolness, lush greenery, mountains and abundant water made it a kind of idealised holiday home for them. Whereas the gardens and palaces elsewhere in their kingdom increasingly expressed their wealth and power, the gardens they made in Kashmir were places of peace and largesse, cool, filled with flowers and, above all, overflowing with water that poured off the hillside from the melting snow down into Lake Dal.

Although Babur had marched into Kashmir in 1528 and sung its praises, it was not conquered by the Mughals until the rule of his grandson Akbar, who first visited in 1589 and subsequently made a road to it through the narrow valley. From that time, while the real business of government took place on the hot, dry plains of Agra and Delhi, Kashmir became a land of relaxation and ease for the Mughal rulers.

It also had its own harvests. The cooler climate meant that apples, pears and plums replaced the citrus and vines of the gardens of the plains. Flowering was not confined to spring, and lilacs, irises, tulips and the saffron crocus flourished.

When the shahs visited Kashmir they would travel to their pleasure gardens on the Dal by boat, and in the first half of the seventeenth century the Vale of Kashmir was said to have 777 gardens on its shores and hillside. The best-known was Shalimar. Begun by Akbar's son and successor Jahangir in 1620 for his wife Nur Jahan, it was completed by Shah Jahan about ten years later. It has two stepped charbaghs descending to an entrance court with a broad central channel down through the levels.

The terraces on which the gardens are made were both a way of using the slope of the hillside and also had important symbolism and practical demarcations for the Mughals. At Shalimar, the emperor gave his audiences on the lower terrace, the central one was semi-private and the top terrace was reserved for the women of the zenana. The central water channel unified them and the charbagh shifted from being based as a square around a central pivot to working along a linear axis as a repeating module, moving from level to level. This provided a model for future gardens both in terms of hydro engineering and design throughout Mughal territory.

❦

OPPOSITE

The Mughal gardens of Kashmir were dominated by water and magnificent chinar, oriental plane, trees.

OPPOSITE
The marble or 'black' pavilion of Shalimar Bagh built by Shah Jahan is in the centre of the ladies' garden set in a basin studded by fountains rising from the water.

RIGHT ABOVE
A broad canal leads down past a pair of summer houses that flank the entrance to the ladies' garden. Today the watercourses only flow completely in spring. This is as a result of deforestation that has led to erosion and a drop in the water table, but in the seventeenth century, when the garden was made, it was endlessly abundant.

BELOW
Looking back up the garden from the Hall of Private Audience.

OVERLEAF
Looking out from the gardens along the banks of Lake Dal with the mountains beyond.

Nishat Bagh

KASHMIR

There is a 1642 painting of Shah Jahan kneeling on a gold carpet in a garden that is itself on a rug of brilliant lapis decorated with brightly coloured flowers, with water tumbling down a chadar, and on either side small rectangular beds filled with flowers. This is Nishat Bagh.

It was built in 1625 by Asaf Khan, a member of the Mughal court inextricably bound into the ruling family. He was the brother of Jahangir's favourite (eighteenth) wife and the father of Mumtaz, wife of Shah Jahan, for whom the Taj Mahal was built; as well as being Shah Jahan's father-in-law he was also his grand vizier.

The terraces were invariably planted with two favourite trees, the cypress (cupressus sempervirens) and chinar (platanus orientalis), the one with its evergreen, columnar form representing life, the other endlessly generous with shade from its huge horizontal branches. The chinars will live to a huge age, and the surviving original trees have another couple of hundred years ahead of them. Both trees are native to Iran and feature significantly in Persian gardens of the same period, forming one of the many links between the Mughals and their distant Persian ancestry.

As with the other gardens along the Dal, the approach was always by boat, and originally the shah's boat could have come right into the garden through a gate from the lake. For such a landlocked culture, this must have been both exciting and exotic as well as heavy with the symbolism of entering paradise from water.

There is a story that when Shah Jahan visited this new garden in 1633, just after Mumtaz's death and as he was beginning work on the Taj Mahal, he was both entranced and deeply jealous. Three times he expressed his extreme admiration, each time hoping that it would prompt Asaf Khan to offer it to him. When no such offer was forthcoming, Shah Jahan, in a fit of thwarted pique, is said to have ordered that the water supply – which came via his own garden of Shalimar Bagh – be closed off. A paradise garden without water is like an English park with withered grass, but Asaf Khan did not dare do anything about it until a servant disobeyed the order. He turned the water back on and life flowed sweetly once again both in the garden and the court.

OPPOSITE
The Mughal gardens of Kashmir were all built on terraces with water running down and along them.

OVERLEAF
A view down the garden terraces to Lake Dal. Nishat Bagh was divided into twelve terraces, to represent the twelve signs of the zodiac, with a central watercourse running through them all.

OPPOSITE
The climate of Kashmir meant that flowers, and thus colour, had a much longer season than in the gardens around Agra and Delhi.

RIGHT ABOVE
Steep chadars mimicked the turbulence of a mountain stream. The result was to take the slopes of the mountains with their rushing water and landscape down the garden terraces and make it orderly without diminishing its energy.

BELOW
Gravity and an abundant water supply meant that the opportunities for the Mughal hydro-engineering skills could be played out to the full.

Pari Mahal

KASHMIR

The Mughals took great pains in choosing the best site for a garden, often going to extreme lengths to bring water to it rather than make a garden where there was a good existing supply of water and compromise on the location. No Mughal garden is more dramatically situated than Pari Mahal which sits 600 feet above the southern shore of Lake Dal in Kashmir, looking across to Akbar's fort on the other side of the water. It was built in 1640 by Dara Shukoh, Shah Jahan's favourite and eldest son, on the site of a Buddhist monastery. It was intended for his tutor Mulla Shah Badakshi, although there is some evidence that Dara Shukoh used it himself as a library. Later, the garden was used as an observatory for teaching both astrology and astronomy and has seven terraces which represent the seven planets.

Of all the gardens in this book, the view – across the lake and out into the skies – is everything. This is a radical departure from the conventional impulse of the Persian paradise garden to look inwards and to be a retreat from the world both of man and hostile nature. Kashmir broke that mould and, as the exception that proved the rule, seems to have been a liberating influence on the Mughals, if perhaps always a departure from the serious business of life.

Communication with other gardens from this elevated site was by pigeon and the biggest building in the garden, among the arcaded walls and arches that line the terraces, is a two-storeyed pigeon house which, like the rest of the buildings and walls, was originally plastered.

Unlike most of the gardens, there is no central water channel down the terraces and thus no cascades or chadars, as water was moved by underground pipes to tanks on the terraces.

Samode Bagh

JAIPUR

The car took me down a long dusty track past goats and chickens, and drew up outside a doorway in a long high wall. Only the smiling faces and uniforms allay the nervousness of being in the wrong place. This is the Samode Bagh, a luxury hotel. The hotel is nice, the food good and the service, as always in India, deeply attentive.

But I am here to see the garden which was made in the 1840s, right at the end of Mughal rule. In fact there had been a garden on this site a hundred years earlier, so this is a continuation of function if not form, because it was created as a summer retreat for the Samode family who were Rajput and Hindi but in the service of the Mughals. Their garden represents the easy marriage between the two cultures and their religions.

It is dramatically based around a central water channel, studded with fountains along its length before it rises up to a large square double pool with jets spraying into the centre from all four sides. Tall trees hold the cool damp air. The water roars and whooshes and splashes as it falls. This is water as drama and entertainment rather than quiet contemplation.

The first two deeply sunken beds of the charbagh are now close-clipped lawn laid out with seats in case mad dogs or this Englishman want to sit out in the midday sun. I resist and head towards the shade of the low and very handsome handsome pavilion at the end of the garden. Further along, the sunken beds on the other side of the central cross path are filled with shrubs and small trees muddled together, and there is a real taste of the authentic Persian planting style of the Mughal charbagh. It is all a bit random and scruffy but that too is authentic. Irrigation of the sunken beds of charbaghs involved flooding them rather than any directed watering, and this encouraged weeds and bare soil in among the fruit trees and flowers in a manner very different from our concept of a well-tended flower bed.

The whole place is a fascinating mixture of Rajput, the British Raj and the last strains of the Mughal Empire, but rather than being a dilution of the purity of the idealised charbagh, it is a tribute to the flexibility and tolerance of the Mughals that they were able to adapt to so much in India.

Despite being an entirely
Hindu Rajput garden,
Samode has the formal
geometry and symmetry of
all Islamic charbaghs.

Looking out from the hotel building with the water rising indoors from the marble floor and out into the gardens.

Pelargoniums in individual terracotta pots line the rill leading down the middle of the garden, flanked by sunken beds.

Despite the clash of styles, with large trees breaking the purity of line and an eclectic mix of planting that reflects its local, British and Mughal influences, Samode is a garden with a distinctly calm atmosphere.

MOROCCO

Visiting Morocco is the closest and easiest way for Europeans to taste the otherness of Africa and a completely different culture. That frisson has been sought out for centuries, but in fact Morocco took a huge amount of its own culture to Spain long before any European tourists reached it, other than the Vandals taking advantage of the collapse of the Roman Empire in the early fifth century.

Morocco is important to the development of paradise gardens both because it had a distinct evolution of architectural and garden design, and also because it was the springboard and source of the Arab invasion of Spain.

Islam arrived in Morocco in 680 with Syrian Umayyad Arabs as part of their westward conquest across the whole of North Africa. In 756 they invaded Spain with largely Berber troops and by the tenth century they ruled the whole of the Iberian peninsula. So the seven hundred years of Islamic influence on Spain that in many ways permeated the whole of European cultural life, stemmed essentially from Morocco – although Morocco itself has always been a mixture of cultures and dynasties, albeit always Islamic from the seventh century onwards.

The European word 'Moors', used to describe the African Arabs, comes from a corruption of 'Mauretania', the Roman name for the area of North Africa that now covers

OPPOSITE

The exotic section of Le Jardin Secret is an exciting blend of modern design, traditional elements and unusual plants from around the world.

RIGHT

Date palms rise above the orchards of the Agdal in Marrakech.

OPPOSITE
*A stork's nest sits atop
the fourteenth-century
minaret tower at the
Chellah in Rabat.*

modern Morocco and Algeria. The Phoenicians, followed by the Carthaginians from modern Tunisia and then the Romans all controlled and passed through Morocco leaving traces of influence, but it was the Berbers, based in the Atlas Mountains, who were the indigenous people.

From its foundation in the eleventh century, Marrakech was a city of gardens. Two-thirds of the medina was orchard or garden and it remained that way until the 1920s. Even today, gardens like Le Jardin Secret exist completely out of view and are entered from the smallest of side streets.

What makes that possible for this city created in the middle of a dry, extremely hot region is the water supply that has brought – and still brings – the melted snow from the Atlas Mountains. There are about 3,000 kilometres of water pipes feeding the city, many of which are over 900 years old and are still in working order. This irrigation system involved an astonishing complexity and sophistication of hydro engineering, comparable, it has been suggested, with the construction of the Egyptian pyramids.

The riad courtyard – enclosed and hidden by high walls so private and protected from sun, wind and dust yet full of light, green shrubs and trees, fruit and flowers and flowing with water – is the archetype of the Moroccan garden. It also tends to follow the formal layout of the charbagh, divided into four equal quarters by water channels or paths with a central fountain, often with a shallow and scalloped basin, and the paths, pillars and walls usually ornamented with the zellij tiles that are found all over the city.

Despite the spread of cheap holidays and the uniform blandness that inevitably accompanies that, Morocco remains thrilling. It is Africa. It is Islam, it is the Atlas Mountains and the Berbers and the long spread of the desert Arab culture that brought so much richness to Europe.

❦

Agdal

The Agdal in Marrakech challenges the broadest interpretation of a garden. It was made in the Almohad era in the second half of the twelfth century and has still not changed significantly. It is huge – over 900 acres – and its name, meaning a walled meadow or garden on the outskirts of a city, comes from the Berber language (the Almohads originated from the Berber tribes of the southern Atlas). There are a number of agdals in Morocco and while the Marrakech Agdal is no meadow, it is surrounded by a wall eight miles long.

Within the wall are vast expanses of orchards centred round two huge basins each about 200 paces square. Despite its size, the combination of fruit laid out in blocks around water that is both a celebration and practical source of irrigation exemplifies all the principles of the paradise garden. Only hundreds of huge carp use the water in the basin today but, as well as being a symbol of abundance, it was the main drinking supply for Marrakech until the nineteenth century and the basins were used to teach the Moroccan army to swim before they ventured across the Strait of Gibraltar. On the far side of the basins are low pavilions that remain open only to the royal family whose palace backs on to the far end of the Agdal.

All the water comes from the distant Atlas Mountains whose craggy outline peeps tantalisingly through the cloud revealing, in winter or spring, snowy peaks. This snow is the source of the water that is collected in wells in the Ourika Valley, and then brought in pipes for over 24 kilometres to channel the snowmelt and provide the city of Marrakech with its main reservoir.

Each orchard is of a single species, with the citrus closest to the basin because they need the most irrigation, and olives, figs, pomegranates and dates stretching into the distance. The gardeners in their blue work suits move around on bicycles, with mattocks over the handlebars, and most of their work involves drawing the loose soil up around the trees so that the water channels to them.

As we leave, skirting the edge of a crumbling gatehouse, a man and small child are selling stale loaves to courting couples so they can photograph each other feeding the writhing shoal of fat carp that snatch at the crumbs with their monstrous mouths.

OPPOSITE
At over 900 acres the Agdal is enormous, but with its central basin surrounded by orchards and the whole area bounded by a wall, it shares all the features of a charbagh a fraction of its size.

OVERLEAF
The central basin of the Agdal contains enough water to fill eighty Olympic swimming pools, all of which is piped from the Atlas Mountains in underground conduits 900 years old.

The Chellah

RABAT

On a hill outside Rabat is the necropolis of Chellah, a tomb garden built between 1310 and 1334 for members of the ruling Merinid family who were then at the peak of their control of the Maghreb. They had overthrown the Almohad caliphate and ruled much of modern Morocco and the kingdom of Granada until they were defeated by the Spanish and Portuguese at the Battle of Salado in 1340, and were finally removed from Morocco in 1465.

Chellah is built on the site of the Roman settlement of Sala Colonia, and among these remains and Merinid graves a gate leads to a five-sided walled enclosure containing royal tombs, two mosques and a religious school or *zawiya*. This is based around a courtyard that has a central rectangular pool, with the familiar brightly coloured patterns of zellij tiles on the floor and walls and scalloped marble basins at either end. A minaret topped with a stork's nest, and also tiled, is in one corner. Despite giving the appearance of a ruined archaeological site, there is evidence that this was a garden, with parterres made around the graves and the zawiya, that combined the symbolism of life and paradise on earth with the tombs of the dead and direct references to the paradise that they were sure to inhabit. Shrubs chosen for their fragrance would have been planted, and these could easily have been irrigated from the water in the courtyard.

The setting of shrines or tombs among gardens was commonplace in the Maghreb, with examples in Marrakech and Tangier, and is found in the siting of Ottoman tombs as well, most famously in the great Mughal tomb gardens of the sixteenth and seventeenth centuries.

The garden of paradise was one of eternal pleasure, eating and drinking 'sweet potions from vessels of silver and goblets of crystal' in the company of dark-eyed houris, and the paradise gardens made among the tombs of the dead would have been similarly sensuous and deliberately conducive to earthly pleasures rather than the solemnity that Christian cemeteries and graveyards almost demand.

What we see today in ruins like Chellah are the dry stones of lost mortality but, in their heyday, they would have created and preserved a living celebration of all that is good in life and in death. Nowhere can this be exemplified more directly than in a garden.

OPPOSITE
Not just the shade, but the colour green itself provides relief from the baking heat.

Traces of ornate tiles surround the repeated horseshoe arches.

A huge tree leans its shade towards the green entrance to the tomb of a marabout, a wandering Sufi holy man.

Palais Lamrani Riad

MARRAKECH

Behind the windowless walls of the narrow streets of the medina in Marrakech and all Moroccan towns, there are hundreds of riads, all with courtyard gardens. They preserved the modesty and privacy of the household and created a place to relax, entertain and enjoy the sensual pleasures of water and green shade, protected from both the human activities of the medina and the heat and hot winds. These interior courtyards also served as a source of light for the buildings when the exterior walls rarely had windows.

All the riad gardens have the same basic pattern of a central fountain and plants in pots, or perhaps a tree or a few shrubs. However, the Palais Lamrani, just five minutes' walk from the Jemaa el Fna, is an example of a riad with a garden that is almost bursting out of its hidden courtyard.

The building was once the early-twentieth-century house of the wealthy Lamrani family from Fez, but was converted – as so many riads in Marrakech have – to an hotel some twenty years ago. The main courtyard is crammed with plants so that the interior space becomes like an overfilled vase with trees growing up the storeys of the building and pushing on out above the roof. A second area, where once carriages were kept, is a now a swimming pool lined in the same deep green tiles used at Le Jardin Secret. More tiles, by the tens of thousands, cover the paths, pillars and walls, still made individually in workshops all over the medina, each tiny section of tile chipped to shape by hand with a hammer, so you have their coolness shaded by an extraordinary lushness, completed by the central fountain that bubbles from its petal-filled basin. The effect, in this parched city, is one of extreme, indulgent luxury.

But it is not the primped, corsetted luxury that one finds in so many modern hotels around the world. Anarchy is only a step away. A fallen palm tree is propped up by a large citrus. Dates, bananas and orange trees fight for light and the upstairs floors have the branches of trees spilling over the parapet like unruly borders. It takes a moment to see through this green tangle that the layout is the traditional charbagh and that this exuberance is another, urban, celebration of the oasis.

ᴡ

OPPOSITE

Looking across the courtyard to what used to be the stable yard which now houses the hotel swimming pool.

OPPOSITE
Rose petals float on the water of the fountain at the centre of the courtyard charbagh. The basin below, the floors and many of the walls are decorated with zellij, the hand-crafted tiny mosaic-like tiles that are such a feature of Moroccan gardens and buildings.

RIGHT
The architectural symmetry and order allows the planting to be spectacularly free and almost anarchic, virtually bursting free from the confines of the courtyard.

Le Jardin Secret

This is a garden hidden behind the narrow streets of the medina that was abandoned before the Second World War but which has recently been restored, redesigned and opened to the public. The site was first built on during the second half of the sixteenth century when it was a small Jewish settlement, however the last occupant died in 1934 and it fell into disrepair until it was bought in 2013 by Lauro Milan. The English designer Tom Stuart-Smith was commissioned to create the garden which he did in two separate but linked parts: the exotic garden and the Islamic garden.

The Islamic garden is a classic charbagh with four sunken beds each subdivided into four, with a shallow scalloped fountain in the centre. The four main intersecting paths are paved with brilliant green tiles, made to match original ones found on site, giving the simultaneous appearance of both water and a cool verdancy. The planting is true, in that it has the simplicity and fruit of a Persian charbagh, but also very modern because it is dominated by stipa tenuissima and subtly interplanted with the mauve flowers of the wild garlic tulbaghia and lavandula dentata. The result is a flowing, easy meadow. When I visited, the stipa had been cut back at random heights giving it a textured appearance of undulating cut-off mounds which was incredibly beautiful and confident in its simplicity.

The exotic garden is connected by a doorway in the corner of the Islamic garden and shares the same rills and pools, but little else. It draws on plants from all over the world to represent the Christian Garden of Eden, and its dark grey walls and Pompeian red pavilion create a strikingly modern and rather austere space crammed with an eclectic mix of plants, in powerful contrast to the simplicity of the charbagh. Of course the plants all share the same ability to grow in this hot, dry climate, and it is their context, crammed together within these high walls, that makes them especially exotic.

The relationship between the two gardens, the contrast with the traditional form of the charbagh and the contemporary planting, plus the luxury of finding a large open space in the cramped confines of the medina filled with just a garden (and a very good cafe), all make this a fine creation, honouring both past and present.

OPPOSITE
The bristly stem of a pachypodium sets the tone of the exotic garden which combines unusual drought-resistant plants from all over the world with the traditional structure of a paradise garden.

OVERLEAF
A view of the Islamic garden from the cafe roof shows its four main beds subdivided again into four, with the green tiles providing both a firm surface and the impression of water.

A crisp rill runs the length
of the exotic garden, from
a pool within the entrance
lobby to the pavilion that
is the transition to the
Islamic garden at the other
end.

RIGHT ABOVE
*The writhing sculptural
forms of the pachypodiums
are just one of the many
shapes and textures
that fill this area with a
dynamic energy.*

BELOW
*The planting of the Islamic
garden is completely
different with clipped stipa
tenuissima interspersed
with the mauve flowers of
the wild garlic, tulbaghia
and lavandula dentata.
It is very simple and
elegantly beautiful.*

LEFT ABOVE
The planting of the exotic garden is dramatically set against high rendered walls that are painted dark grey or a delicate pink, with the pavilion a strong Pompeian red.

BELOW
The sunken beds of the Islamic garden are edged with a clipped hedge of fastigiate rosemary providing structure and rich fragrance.

OPPOSITE
Dasylirion acrotrichum is a native of the Chihuahuan Desert in Mexico, but very happy under the Marrakech sun.

Umberto Pasti Garden

TANGIER

Tangier still retains its seedy glamour, close enough to Europe to be handy and to cock a snook but far enough culturally, morally and physically to cast off the restrictions that shackle free spirits. It is a place where the forbidden is condoned and the disregarded allowed to flourish, and where strangers are allowed to belong without surrendering their strangeness.

The garden of Umberto Pasti, novelist and gardener, on the hills just above the city, is a kind of paradigm of the aesthetic style of ex-pat Tangier. It is understated and natural, yet filled with beautiful things choreographed and orchestrated by a master. Pasti's preference is for gardens that look as though they have had no gardener, and that appear unshaped. However, I know that this takes as much skill as – and often more than – licking a garden into shape. Pasti began by collecting rare bulbs threatened by development and planted them in his garden which, literally, grew from there. The result is rather like his house, a patchwork of rare and exquisite things thrown together to look as though they have fallen without any artifice at all. As well as a collection of over 5,000 species of plants, there is water: bubbling from a broad scalloped dish and in a long pool. Pasti says he especially likes frogs so he has to have water – a slightly tangential take on the life-giving properties of water in the paradise garden.

There are three pavilions, the third erected about fifteen years ago when Pasti bought the plot below his house to stop anyone spoiling his view. He commissioned Roberto Peregalli and Laura Rimini to build a new 'old' pavilion as though it had always been there, using materials salvaged from demolished homes. The result is a tribute to the buildings of the Moroccan past. Pasti feels strongly about conserving that heritage, and trains young men from the nearby village to make furniture and to garden so they are employable and can help maintain the gardens he designs for clients.

His gardening philosophy is to tap into the inner child and let it play. What results will, he believes, by default be beautiful. This sidelines the key role of the meticulous collector and plantsman scrupulously tending and adjusting house and garden, but there is clearly sufficient adult expertise on hand to let the inner child roam free.

❧

OPPOSITE
Carpets have always been an important feature of the paradise garden, both representing its spring flowers and as the preferred surface to sit upon. Here flowers, stone and terracotta harmonise perfectly with the faded tones of the carpet on the wall behind.

OPPOSITE
The garden, like the house,
is a collection of beautiful
things falling artlessly
together – via Umberto
Pasti's very particular
guiding hand.

RIGHT
Simply a pot in a bowl in a
window within an Islamic
horseshoe arch. Simply
beautiful.

Le Jardin Majorelle

MARRAKECH

After the First World War Marrakech became a favoured resort of liberal French artists including Jacques Majorelle who came for health reasons in 1917 and stayed. In 1924 he bought the plot of land that Le Jardin Majorelle is built on, and in 1931 he began to make a garden and studio for himself. He painted the building and pots the intense Berber blue that he had seen in the Atlas Mountains, immediately creating a dramatic and radically daring backdrop to the plants that he began to collect obsessively.

Majorelle died in 1962 but his plant collection remains, and in 1981 the fashion designer Yves St Laurent and his partner Pierre Bergé bought the abandoned house and garden, and the American garden designer Madison Cox restored and revamped it. Yves St Laurent died in 2008 and Pierre Bergé in 2017, but since 2011 the garden has been owned by the Fondation Majorelle and remains open to the public.

Every garden has its own qualities and character but Majorelle is truly unique. The combination of the matt depth of the paint colours – dominated by the Berber blue, also the yellow and green of the pots – and the intensity of the planting is quite unlike anywhere else I have visited. The planting is remarkable in both its abundance and peculiarity, as Jaques Majorelle's beloved cacti, succulents and palms are displayed like models on a catwalk parading their outfits, each daring the eye to look away. Many of these plants are placed as individual specimens in gravel, each one holding a pose, but it is the interplay between them that is so extraordinary and beautiful – unless you are a botanist or collector admiring them for what they are rather than what they look like. But the garden is not a series of static poses. The vertical energy of the palms, bamboos and cacti and the intensity of the planting, added to the colour, means that this is high-octane stuff. The water running in the channels and fountains is cooling and soothing, but it cannot tone down the garden's vibrancy.

This is a garden made by European Christians in Islamic Africa with a deliberate sense of freedom from the constraints of any social, artistic or religious boundaries. The energy that is created is electric, yet it still honours and respects all the Islamic elements that have gone into its creation.

A pergola made from
bound bamboos adds
formal structure.

RIGHT ABOVE
The distinct Berber blue
runs through the garden on
all walled surfaces and is
made all the bluer by the
contrasting chrome yellow
pots.

BELOW
The lily pond is framed
with luxuriant planting.

LEFT ABOVE
One of the many joys of the garden is the way that shapes and silhouettes carve themselves from the air making the garden abstract and, at times, surreal.

BELOW
The edges of the raised rill run like electric blue tramlines through the garden.

OPPOSITE
A private section of the garden.

OVERLEAF
Jacques Majorelle made a collection of cacti, succulents and palms and these still form the core of the modern garden, creating an extraordinary ballet of extreme botanic form.

OPPOSITE
Cacti thrust skyward and the palms explode in bursts of leaf high above them.

RIGHT ABOVE
The garden has nothing natural about it, from the dream-like intensity of the painted surfaces, the gravelled ground and the mixture of plants, yet it has an internal logic and harmony that gives it poise and balance.

BELOW
An arcade flanked by the flower spikes of acanthus mollis is surprisingly conventional.

SPAIN

THE INFLUENCE OF CATHOLIC SPAIN ON EUROPE AND ITS EMPIRE
IN the Americas tends to suppress the significance of Islam and the longevity of the
Moorish empire. The Moors – so called because they came from Mauretania, the name
that the Romans gave to modern Morocco – first crossed the Strait of Gibraltar in 711.
They were part of the Umayyad caliph whose capital was Damascus, and whose empire
extended across North Africa, the Arabian peninsula, modern Iran, Iraq, Afghanistan, the
Punjab, the Mediterranean and the Middle East. By 756 they controlled the area south of
Córdoba, and by the tenth century the whole of Spain and modern Portugal was under
Muslim rule.

We used to dismiss the period between 410 AD and 1066 as the Dark Ages, with the
post-Roman world sliding into barbarism. That view is now discredited, and we know
that the picture, although scantily recorded, was complex and often culturally rich. What
is certain, however, is that by the tenth century there was a social, architectural, legal,
engineering, agricultural, philosophical and artistic culture in Islamic Spain that was
more advanced and sophisticated than anywhere else in contemporary Europe.

Córdoba, the Moorish capital in this early period, was renowned for its schools,
libraries, mathematicians and philosophers, and was effectively the intellectual centre

OPPOSITE
Towering pillars of cypress
create dramatic green
architecture at the Urquijo
Garden in Toledo.

RIGHT
The garden of the Real
Alcázar in Seville is a
combination of Moorish
and Spanish styles.

of Europe. This was an inclusive, highly tolerant, largely secular society where Muslim, Jewish and Christian communities could coexist under Arab rule.

Gardens were an important part of that culture and there was considerable horticultural and botanical knowledge with the introduction of plants that remain such a key part of the southern European gardens and diet such as oranges, lemons, peaches, apricots, figs, dates, ginger and pomegranate, as well as rice, saffron and sugar cane. Added to that was a sophisticated understanding of hydro engineering, bringing water miles across parched landscapes, that meant that paradise gardens were an essential part of wealthy Moorish buildings.

One of the reasons that southern Spain attracted the Islamic invasion is that its climate and landscape is most like that of the desert Arabs who introduced the Islamic religion and culture. It was then, as now, a place of furious heat but also with highly fertile land. It was accessible across a stretch of water barely ten miles wide, and for 700 years – longer than Spain has been a wholly Christian country – it felt like home.

The influence of the Moors was immersive and remains so to this day. By the thirteenth century the Mudejar culture was strong, where Islamic architecture, design, motifs and, in particular, building techniques and skills were entwined with Christian design and use in a harmonious and deliberate way. In the gardens of the Real Alcázar in Seville, for example, it is hard – and largely unhelpful – to disentangle the Islamic from the Christian. Both cultures are enriched and expanded.

But the Umayyad dynasties declined, Al-Andalus (Islamic Spain) broke into small kingdoms, and although it came together again under the Berber Almoravids this did not last long. Gradually the whole peninsula came under Catholic control until the Alhambra was the last bastion to fall and the last Moor, the Nasrid King Boabdil, on 2 January 1492 officially surrendered control of the peninsula to the Catholic Ferdinand and Isabella of Castile and left Spain for Morocco.

Eight months later Christopher Columbus set sail across the Atlantic having been granted permission and sponsorship from Ferdinand and Isabella. Spain and the world, old and new, were changing absolutely.

❦

The Alhambra

GRANADA

The Alhambra is now a huge tourist attraction and you join thousands of others even before the doors open. But it has always been a heavily populated, busy place, more a small fortified town than a palace. The first buildings on the site were built in the middle of the thirteenth century by al-Ahmar, the first Nasrid king, but the greatest period of development was during the rule of Emir Muhammad V, in the second half of the fourteenth century. Existing buildings were remodelled and new palaces butted up against and into them, the ensemble edging and adjusting as it went. But it is the gardens that truly bind together the buildings that contain them. You zigzag, seemingly slipping through side doors and alleyways, from the palaces of the Mexuar, Comares, Court of the Lions and the Partal Gardens. This sense of gardens being hidden within buildings would have been much greater in the Alhambra's heyday because many buildings have disappeared, and their presence is now marked only by gardens – the walls becoming hedges, corridors paths and rooms patios or borders. These surviving gardens are the oldest Islamic gardens in Europe and among the most complete medieval gardens in the world, offering a unique insight into the Moorish civilisation that dominated Spain for 700 years.

Across the valley is the summer palace of the Generaliffe, its long terraces punctuated with cypresses and the iconic courtyard lined with arcing jets. This courtyard, with its central canal linking the pavilions at either end and flowers carpeting the sunken beds, has a satisfying familiarity, and indeed the Generaliffe gardens, with their cypress walks, roses and terraced vegetable beds, are the most accessible for modern Western visitors. But the rest of the gardens, from the gleaming marble surfaces of the Court of the Lions to the goldfish-glinting waters in front of the Partal, all make sense when you consider that they were intended to be enjoyed when seated on a carpet woven from the finest wool or silk, with music playing softly as the light fell and the night cooled. These were gardens of luxury and delight, and their seclusion was integral to that.

Yet there is sadness to the Alhambra. The morning of 2 January 1492 when Boabdil, Abu Abdallah Muhammad XII, the last sultan of Granada, rode with his attendants in their full finery to surrender to Ferdinand and Isabella of Castile was the end of the old order. The poet Lorca said that when the last Moors were driven from Spain they took with them a lightness of spirit and a tolerance that have never been reclaimed.

✿

OPPOSITE

The Alhambra is a series of palaces that connect and open into each other, and each with its own garden.

OVERLEAF

Many buildings have disappeared and their presence is now marked by gardens, the walls becoming hedges, corridors paths and rooms patios or borders.

The decorative detail of the
buildings is as intense as
the finest lacework, and
although the delicacy and
subtlety of the light seems
perfect to the modern
eye, originally all the
plasterwork would have
been as brightly painted as
the surviving tiles.

RIGHT

The courtyard of the
Generaliffe, with its
arching fountains lining
the central canal and the
sunken beds filled with a
carpet of flowers, is one
of the most visited and
famous gardens of the
world.

LEFT ABOVE

Artichokes growing in rows – a lot of the vegetables and fruit for the Moorish court were always grown on site on the terraces that are still used for vegetables.

BELOW

The greatest luxury under the burning sun is cool green – be it of water, hedge or the shade of a tree.

OPPOSITE

The Generaliffe gardens amount to much more than the iconic courtyard and were largely laid out in the 1930s in the Moorish style and spirit.

OVERLEAF

Looking across from the Generaliffe, the Alhambra is a small city linked by a series of exquisite gardens and buildings containing extraordinary riches.

Real Alcázar

Walk into the courtyard of the Real Alacázar on an early spring morning and you will be overwhelmed by the bouquet of a hundred orange trees bearing thousands of delicate cream flowers that fill the surrounding streets with an astonishing intensity of scent. As you go into this most fragrant of royal palaces, the bells of the neighbouring cathedral toll from its Giralda tower. This was built to call the faithful to prayer and is as visible a symbol as any of the entwined Islamic and Christian history of Seville.

Although there was a fortress on the site dating from the tenth century, it was substantially rebuilt in the 1360s by Pedro the Cruel. Pedro was undoubtedly vindictive and murderous, but he also embraced the Muslim world and his building was a deliberate example of the Mudejar, where Christian and Islamic styles sit comfortably together.

The centre of the complex and the most pure surviving Islamic garden is the Patio de las Doncellas, or Court of the Maidens. This was covered with marble slabs for 500 years, but in 2007 it was restored to its original layout with deeply sunken beds, bounded by ornate intertwining brick arches, flanking a long canal lined in blue tiles. The orange trees in these beds are at head height as you stroll by the side of the rill, the flowers inches from your nose and the fruits within easy plucking reach. Double pillars colonnade the surrounding walls laced with intricate Mudejar plasterwork. This is a pure paradise garden, filled with water, flowers, fruit, birdsong and shade, surrounded with exquisite plasterwork and tiles – all made for a Spanish Christian king.

Nothing else at the Alcázar appears so apparently Islamic, yet the series of gardens, both within the palace and in the park, have evolved from intimate, enclosed Islamic spaces to gardens designed for courtiers to parade. Although the rills still run, fountains have lost their bubbling modesty and become grand and ornate, and the main water feature, the Estanque de Mercurio, that was once a Moorish reservoir backed by the palace wall, is now fed by a stream of water jetting dramatically from the roof and the old wall is made into a loggia embellished and encrusted like an Italianate Renaissance grotto.

The changes layer one on the other and are all part of the character of this extraordinary palace and gardens. But what remains after water and stone shapeshift through the centuries, swirling Moorish, Mudejar and Mannerist elements together, is the lingering memory of the fragrance of orange blossom.

OPPOSITE

The garden of the Real Alcázar is as much a combination of Moorish and later Christian styles as the Mudejar architecture of the buildings.

PARADISE GARDENS

ABOVE
*Cypresses were much used
by the Moors but clipping
them into solid green walls
is a much later, Spanish
horticultural style.*

Seville has a long history
of hand-painted tiles
which are not just highly
decorative because
they also provide an
exceptionally durable
surface perfectly adapted
to counter the city's high
humidity.

LEFT
Clipped myrtle and box hedges contain little orchards of bitter Seville oranges in the Jardín de Las Damas which was redesigned in the sixteenth century for the marriage of Charles V and Isabella of Portugal, and in doing so converted the Islamic garden into a space for courtiers to promenade.

OVERLEAF
The Patio de las Doncellas is the perfect example of Mudejar architecture and, since its restoration in 2004, of a paradise garden with its central long basin and deeply sunken beds planted with orange trees so the blossom and fruits are at exactly face height as you stroll past them.

Urquijo Garden (Palacio de Galiana)

TOLEDO

As well as being the home of El Greco and famous for the manufacture of the best swords and daggers in Europe, Toledo was the centre for botanical studies in Al-Andalus, and in the eleventh century had a botanical garden founded by the pharmacist Ibn Wafid, vizier to Al-Mamun, King of Toledo (1043–75).

The Palace of Galiana – named after the Muslim princess married to Charlemagne – was built originally by Al-Mamun as an *almunia*, or place of pleasure (as opposed to a place of government), outside the town walls by the banks of the Tagus River. In fact the palace did not last long as it was razed during the Almoravid siege of Toledo in the early twelfth century, and began a long history of changing ownership and use, spending time as a palace, monastery and home.

In 1959 it was purchased by Manuel Gómez-Moreno and his wife Carmen Marañón and carefully restored to the point that it retains its grandeur and structure without being modernised in any way, with a lovely garden laid out among the walls and ruins. Today this garden is dominated by soaring spires of cypress planted like green colonnades before the old building, enclosing and screening it to create the privacy so essential to the original garden of Al-Mamun and yet, in a manner contrary to the ideals of outward modesty and an inward, contemplative stance central to the gardens of Islam, it is loudly, visibly dramatic.

The relationship between ruined buildings and gardens is always rich with possibility, especially if the ruins retain nobility and the gardens are vibrantly well maintained. The juxtaposition of buildings, their apparent emptiness heavy with distant centuries of humanity, and a garden, clipped, ordered and only fully alive in the present is always powerful. One of the features of any garden created amidst ruins is that it inevitably feels like a magnificent stage set waiting for the actors to bring it to life. Every garden needs people to trigger it into being. An empty garden is unknowable, or at least can only be guessed at. But what makes walking in a garden among the ghosts and memories of buildings so moving is the awareness of all those feet that have trodden this way before. History comes alive in a way that the unoccupied stones never can.

OPPOSITE
The extraordinary pencil-thin shape of the cypress, cupressus sempervirens, forms a dramatic and spectacular cluster that no other tree could create.

RIGHT ABOVE
The building is roofless and not used but has been carefully restored to provide a thousand-year-old structure to frame the modern garden.

BELOW
Terracotta plant pots on plinths, steps and hung from the stone walls add a touch of domesticity.

OVERLEAF
Irises bake in the spring sun with the proud shell of the building making a magnificent backdrop.

ABOVE
Olives are tended and
harvested in the garden
just as they would have
been in the eleventh
century when it was first
made.

The silhouette of an Islamic horseshoe arch is a reminder of the garden's Moorish past, while the extraordinary cypresses are wrapped like figures cloaked in green.

TURKEY

As a schoolboy I had to learn a series of fifty supposedly seminal, but actually quite random, dates known as 'specials'. One of these was the Fall of Constantinople whose date is still, fifty years later, etched on my memory as 1453.

This was when the Ottomans, by dint of one of the first sieges to use gunpowder successfully to overcome city defences, finally took the great city that had been capital of the Byzantine Empire for the past 1,500 years. As well as the impact that this had on European and military history, it also meant that Constantinople was now Muslim and that the Ottoman Empire was consolidated and centred around this new capital. At its peak in the seventeenth century, it ranged across much of the Muslim world, around Arabia, along North Africa, up through the Middle East and over what is now modern Greece, Hungary and almost right round to the Black Sea. This empire lasted for over 450 years until Mustafa Kemal Atatürk ended it in 1922.

The Ottoman period of greatest power coincided with the rise of the Safavids in Persia and the Mughals in India, modern Pakistan and Afghanistan. These three great powers were all descended from or connected to Timur, or Tamerlane, the scion of the Mongolian warrior leader Genghis Khan and responsible, it is claimed, for the deaths of over seventeen million people in the name of Islam. Despite this common line of descent

OPPOSITE
Kiosks are the key element of all Ottoman gardens, although not all are as substantial or ornamental as this one in the Topkapi Palace in Istanbul.

RIGHT
The Ottomans carefully selected sites for their gardens that had a view over water.

OPPOSITE
*Istanbul has always
been the meeting place
of European and Asian
cultures and religions.*

all three had quite distinct cultures – and at times both the Ottomans and the Mughals were at war with the Safavids – that were reflected in the way that they made and used their gardens.

Constantinople had been the centre of Byzantine Christianity, but after the conquest of the city Istanbul became the centre of an Islamic caliphate. However, its relationship with the natural world was very different from either that of the desert Arabs or the Persians. Whereas the traditional charbagh was enclosed, hidden and protected behind plain high walls, and the garden within an ecstatic celebration of the water and greenery that was so absent from the desert around it, the Ottomans celebrated and wished to include and enjoy the natural world around them. They would carefully site their palaces and gardens so that they had good views of rivers and lakes and did not try to screen them off, enjoying what we would now call a borrowed landscape. These natural water features took the role of the more elaborate formal water in Arabian and Persian gardens and yet, as an element of the gardens, they were just as important.

This means that Ottoman gardens are much more Western in style than other paradise gardens although, like every aspect of Istanbul and the Ottoman Empire, the cultural mix is based firmly on Islamic beliefs and behaviour. Nevertheless, just as modern Turkey remains caught between two strong and sometimes conflicting cultures, there was a well-developed interplay with Renaissance ideas from Europe that was never suppressed or ignored but was underscored by the Greco-Roman inheritance from the long period when Byzantium was the centre of the eastern Roman Empire.

Topkapi Palace

ISTANBUL

Within a couple of years of taking Constantinople and thus securing complete control over his vast Ottoman kingdom, Mehmet II moved the royal palace and built a new one on the site of an old Greco-Roman building on the Seraglio Point with a magnificent view over the Bosphorus and the Sea of Marmara. This was to be the centre of government as well as royal life for the next 400 years, and visitors described large gardens within the palace grounds with orchards and meadows and a limitless supply of fresh water.

The palace takes the form of three progressively exclusive courtyards, the gardens associated with each becoming less park-like and more formal. Over the evolution and construction of the palace (which took over 400 years) the major difference from the contemporary Persian and Mughal gardens is that the love of tight geometry and formal symmetry was eschewed in favour of natural topography and the influence and welcome inclusion of the surrounding landscape. There was also a belief in animism that held every living thing sacred, and this especially applied to the trees in the Topkapi Palace. Some of the modern-day cypresses and planes pre-date the Ottomans and are revered in their hollowed-out monolithic majesty.

Suleyman the Magnificent (1520–66) apparently employed 2,600 gardeners who tended thousands of roses, bulbs and cypresses. I suspect that barely one in a hundred of those gardeners remains today. However, the garden is still planted with huge blocks of roses and features that most Ottoman of all garden buildings: the kiosk.

When the anglophone mind thinks of a kiosk, it is inevitably a seaside shack selling newspapers, ice creams or bad sweets, or a bandstand in a dismal corner of a public park. But the true kiosk is a fine pavilion that can go from intimate to palatial, and kiosks were key elements in both how Ottoman gardens were used, as well as how they looked. Their interiors in the Topkapi Palace are magnificent, adorned with fireplaces, finely cushioned divans and carpets and arguably the most beautiful floral tiles ever produced. Kiosks were places to sit, to receive guests, to hear music and poetry and to govern. The Topkapi Palace accumulated a number of kiosks over the years and the garden accommodated and absorbed them, in keeping with the spirit of adapting and accepting the natural world rather than rigidly shaping it.

❦

LEFT ABOVE & BELOW
Some of the most exquisite ceramic tiles ever made are the sixteenth-century floral decorations of tulips and carnations on the walls of the Circumcision Room. The tulips show the long, elegant flowers favoured by the Ottomans.

OPPOSITE
The palace is set on the Seraglio Point above the Sea of Marmara as it enters the Bosphorus Strait and looks out across to Asia.

The fourth courtyard was the inner sanctuary of the sultan and his family and has a succession of kiosks added over the years. It was once forbidden to all outsiders but is now the most visited part of the Topkapi.

Emirgan Park

ISTANBUL

On the wooded banks of the Bosphorus, colour reeled and romped and cavorted in every shade of carnival excess and then, fearing itself to be too restrained and tasteful, ratcheted it all up several notches and *really* went to town. If the great ribbons of three million tulips blazoned between the trees were not enough, there was a full-size river of brilliant blue grape hyacinths with banks of chrome yellow and vermilion, and swans made from white tulips gliding stately by.

We had come to witness the tulip festival held in the park each April. It was kitsch, brash and challenged every notion of good taste. I was not so much disapproving as in a state of shock. However, the locals came out in their tens of thousands to adore it, and wedding couples queued to have their photographs taken in front of the most lurid tableaux.

The Ottomans loved tulips and they were particularly popular in the court of Suleyman the Magnificent, the sultan of the great Ottoman Empire from 1520 till 1566. Tulips were introduced to Vienna in 1554 and then to Holland in 1593 when the first bulbs were planted in Leiden. Within a quarter of a century people became besotted with them and 'tulip mania' quickly took hold. In a frenzy of forward buying, bulbs changed hands at staggering prices. In the early 1630s a single bulb of a rare or exotic tulip cost about three times the annual wage of a skilled manual worker, or about the same price as a smart Amsterdam townhouse. This meant that they were worth many times more than their weight in gold. Significantly, it was not the flowers that were being bought but the bulbs, on the off-chance that they would 'break' and have the characteristic smudging and streaking on their petals that we now know is caused by a virus, spread by an aphid. The tulip bubble inevitably burst, but the love of full, blowsy tulips has never left the spectrum of European taste.

The Ottomans, however, loved a much more refined, elongated, elegant form of tulip – rather more like the modern acuminata – as portrayed on the sublime Iznik tiles of the period. One can but wonder what Suleyman would have made of Emirgan Park in full twenty-first-century bloom!

OPPOSITE
Emirgan Park in spring with the first touches of blossom and fresh foliage opening above the tulips.

ABOVE
Three million tulips flower simultaneously each spring in the park. For once the cliché 'a riot of colour' is supremely apt.

RIGHT
*When we were in the park
dozens of brides came
to have their wedding
pictures taken, resulting
in a breathtaking
and, at times, baffling
combination of charm and
kitsch!*

ENGLAND

THERE ARE 2.4 MILLION MUSLIMS LIVING IN BRITAIN AND ISLAM IS the second largest religion. Given that gardening is the most popular pastime and some ninety per cent of households have access to a garden, it is not unreasonable to suppose that a fair number of British Muslims are keen gardeners. However, compared to the rest of the population, the Muslim community is demographically very young – in 2010 over half were under twenty-five – and there is a tendency for gardening to appeal to the home-owning middle aged with the time to enjoy it. Also, the majority of British Muslims came from rural communities in Pakistan, Bangladesh and India. The association with the land as being directly connected to poverty and back-breaking work is a close one, and bettering oneself and integrating successfully into British society has tended to mean a rejection of all manual work – even recreational.

But that is slowly changing. Many allotments in cities like Birmingham, Leeds or Bradford have a high representation of Asian allotmenteers, and as immigrants become successful and own houses they take on gardens and – to some extent – gardening too. The Islamic influence from Spain has always been less potent than that of Renaissance Italy or France, but the British involvement in India, first via the East India Company and then through the Raj, meant that Mughal gardens began to be copied. Sezincote in the

OPPOSITE
The green of the grass in Bradford's Mughal Garden is at odds with the elements of shade and coolness from a burning desert sun, but the charbagh is merely adapted, not lost.

RIGHT
Despite their very English summer borders, the gardens at Hestercombe, Somerset, show Islamic influences.

*Soft pink roses and their
terracotta pots harmonise
with the pink walls of the
Prince of Wales's Carpet
Garden at Highgrove.*

Cotswolds, built at the beginning of the nineteenth century, is the most famous example but, with its mingling Islamic and Hindu images, its style might be classed as Oriental rather than Islamic.

Two hundred years later, the Mughal Garden at Bradford and the Carpet Garden at Highgrove both appeared at the same time, albeit quite independently of each other. Both are accessible to the public to some extent. The former was made by a council with lottery money and the latter by a royal prince, its first incarnation being as an exhibit at the Chelsea Flower Show before being relocated to its present home at Highgrove. Both are exceptional and unusual.

The central question regarding paradise gardens in Britain seems to be deciding who they are for. Are they a way of making a large immigrant minority feel at home (as though they need a place they can go to that feels culturally comfortable)? Or are they simply an expression of a gardening style that, like many others, can be extremely beautiful?

Both questions are fraught with problems. The first makes assumptions that immigrant communities have to be fed ersatz reminders of 'home', even though the vast majority of their members will have been born and raised here. The second question is slightly more puzzling. The only truly British style of gardening is the landscape movement of the mid eighteenth century and that is, as it always was, laughably inaccessible to the vast majority of householders. All other styles of gardening are derivative, so why have we British not derived more from Islamic paradise gardens? Do we need some knowledge of the Koran or empathy with Islam to appreciate them? Or is it just a cultural blind spot in the range of gardens that we make and enjoy?

One would hope that the resolution of these two things would increase the number of paradise gardens being made in Britain: so Muslims can make them as a deliberate choice of design and as one of the expressions of their faith, and that non-Muslims use the idioms and examples from around the Islamic world to broaden the range of gardens that we British who are – above all – a nation of garden lovers, can share and enjoy.

Hestercombe

TAUNTON

Hestercombe House was the home of the Hon. Edward and Lady Portman who, in 1903, commissioned an up-and-coming young architect to design a new formal garden on the sloping ground beyond the Victorian terrace in front of the house.

That architect's name was Edwin Lutyens, and at the age of age of thirty-four, as well as his idiosyncratic style of Arts and Crafts houses, he had begun his relationship with Gertrude Jekyll designing gardens. Lutyens did the layout and hard landscaping and she supplied the planting plans. Eventually they were to work on over a hundred gardens together although Hestercombe was one of their earlier collaborations. In all his correspondence about the garden over the four years of its construction, Lutyens never once mentioned any Islamic inspiration, yet I would suggest that Hestercombe is one of the best examples of how the Islamic paradise garden has shaped and influenced British garden design. Lutyens's garden is essentially a square charbagh, deeply sunken below the Victorian terrace leading from the house, with raised walkways on two sides and a raised pergola across the bottom. The central plat is divided diagonally into four with a central urn rather than a fountain.

Water is the key. It runs along the side walkways in rills, just like the channels found in all paradise gardens from Cyrus's Pasargadae to the late Mughal gardens in India. Water flows gently into pools and is then fed into those rills, the floors of which are set with stone on edge to create a rippling effect – just like the pigeon-breast carving on Persian and Kashmiri cascades. The water then drops down a series of steps into pools. There is a still, circular pond in an octagonal stone-lined rotunda, the intricacy of stone providing both a harmony and complexity that is reminiscent of the pavilions of Persian and Mughal gardens.

Although water is an essential element in the garden, Lutyens used grass in such a way that it acts as a water substitute. He made long strips of grass edged with stone and then bounded by borders that are too wide to be considered paths, but yet too narrow to qualify as lawns. Visually they work exactly as the canals and basins in gardens like Hasht Behest in Isfahan or the Generaliffe at the Alhambra.

The only lasting regret at Hestercombe is that the Portmans did not demolish the ugly house and ask Lutyens to design a new one worthy of his garden.

OPPOSITE

Gertrude Jekyll is rightly celebrated for her planting plans such as this at Hestercombe, but the real gardening genius lay in Edwin Lutyens's design.

OPPOSITE

Lutyens's use of rills that then ran down into pools is taken directly from paradise gardens, especially those in India.

ABOVE

Hestercombe is essentially a huge sunken bed divided into four equal parts like a charbagh, albeit on the diagonal and with an urn rather than a fountain at its centre.

Mughal Garden

LISTER PARK, BRADFORD

The Mughal Garden in Bradford was made as part of the restoration of Lister Park in an attempt to reflect the culture of the strong local Asian community. Lister Park was originally the home of the Lister family until 1870 when Samuel Cunliffe Lister sold Manningham Park, as it was then called, to Bradford Corporation for half its value on condition that it be used as an art gallery and the grounds made into a public park. The house was demolished and the current Cartwright Hall was built in its place, but at the end of the twentieth century the park had become run-down and locals felt unsafe using it. Over four million pounds was raised to redevelop it and, as part of the process, a former car park was made into a Mughal paradise garden.

However, rather than being divided into the four equal sections based around a water feature, the garden is rectangular and has a central canal with a round pond and fountain furthest from the house and, opposite it, a square moated platform with a fountain at its centre surrounded by a large expanse of paving. It is built into a cross slope, so from two sides you look down on the garden, with trees and hedging enclosing the other two sides.

I visited on an overcast summer Sunday morning and although the grass and hedges were very green under the northern sky, the York stone paving was grey and the water – so important for cooling and refreshing the baking air in Lahore or Agra – looked freezing cold. All in all, the Mughal Garden was admirable but uninviting.

But then a wonderful thing happened. The park gradually became busy and the garden filled with families. Some picnicked, not on carpets as they might have done in Isfahan but on benches and with the same kind of elaborate meals and gas stoves for making tea. Others walked, men in fine white kurtas, women in varying degrees of traditional dress but, above all, there were children.

Children running, children playing, children bewitched by water. They jumped across it, patted and slapped the fountains, splashed through it and danced around it. Such, such were their joys, and the solemnity of the Mughal Garden, designed and maintained by committee and set out for the good of community like a stage, was made to dance – for what would paradise be without children?

❧

OPPOSITE

Just as it is in every paradise garden, water, channelled and controlled with fountains, rills and basins, is the key element in the Bradford Mughal Garden.

OVERLEAF

The garden is made on the site of a former car park and designed to allow plenty of room for people to walk, meet, picnic and for their children to play safely, making it a truly communal space used in a way very similar to public gardens in Iran.

Carpet Garden, Highgrove

TETBURY

OPPOSITE

The Carpet Garden is surrounded by a high wall of local Cotswold stone, rendered on the inside, to create the privacy and modesty of a traditional courtyard charbagh.

OVERLEAF

The centrepiece of the Carpet Garden is a fountain bowl carved in Granada from a single piece of white marble weighing over a ton. This is set on an octagonal plinth decorated with fifty-six differently shaped tiles especially made for the garden.

The Carpet Garden at Highgrove, the Prince of Wales's home in Gloucestershire, was originally designed and constructed for the Chelsea Flower Show in 2001. The idea for it came from the prince himself, based upon a pair of Anatolian tribal carpets in his possession. Carpets are an essential feature of all Islamic gardens from Cyrus's time to the present day, and the finer ones were often conceived as 'gardens' that could be sat on outside in the summer months and indoors in winter, bringing the spring-flowering garden with you. So making a garden from a carpet that could be laid out at Chelsea and then rolled up and brought back to Highgrove has a neatly cyclical pattern.

The garden is a classic charbagh with a raised fountain in its centre, spilling into a broad, scalloped marble basin and surrounded with a plinth and steps decorated with Moroccan zellij tiles. I first saw it at Highgrove a few years after it was installed, when it looked slightly ill at ease – it seemed in place but not at home. But I visited again recently and the garden, now sixteen years old, was transformed both literally and in feel.

You enter through a wooden door in a blank wall and enter immediately an enclosed, jewelled space, rich in colour and texture. The walls that lend the sense of a Middle Eastern courtyard are a lovely apricot colour and are complemented by terracotta pots filled with pink and red roses and peach-coloured terracotta tiles on the paths. The roses are a recent addition and transform the garden and, along with generous billows of herbaceous geraniums, add a prettiness that sits easily with the rigidity of the structure and strength of green. It is as though this rather pure, austere idea has been allowed to breathe and express itself in the language that it feels comfortable with – which is that of an English country garden blended almost perfectly with a Middle Eastern charbagh.

There is a lesson here. Making a perfect replica of any particular style of garden can only take you so far. It always becomes an academic exercise but rarely with the heart and soul every garden must have. What the Carpet Garden at Highgrove has acquired through time and good gardening is that essential quality of charm.

OPPOSITE
A superb cork oak provides height and texture in what is now an established garden that feels and looks at ease with itself in this very English setting.

RIGHT ABOVE
The plants used have evolved over the years but they still reflect the carpets that were the original inspiration for the garden.

BELOW
Many of the roses are later additions that give the garden a softness and sense of place despite the very strong Islamic influence. The orange trees are grown in pots so they can be taken in over winter for protection.

Acknowledgements

I SHOULD LIKE TO THANK THE PATIENT AND EXTREMELY LONG-suffering work and advice of Lisa Highton, Caroline Westmore and Amanda Jones at Two Roads as well as the superb work of Andrew Barron in designing this book.

My agent Alexandra Henderson has been a rock, gentle goad and good friend as well as an ideal companion on visits to the gardens in Spain, India and England.

Wherever we went we had help and guidance for which I am extremely grateful to many people in many countries to gain access, often privileged, to these gardens. But I should especially like to thank Farzad Pak who made our all-too-brief time in Iran so memorable and successful.

Travelling and working with Derry Moore has been one of the highlights of my professional and private life. We have had good adventures.

Finally, and most importantly, I must thank my wife Sarah for sharing and making our own *pairidaeza*.

Monty Don

IN A BOOK OF THIS NATURE, THERE ARE MANY PEOPLE TO whom I, as the photographer, am indebted, and I hope that anyone I may have neglected to thank will forgive me.

Firstly I would like to thank Señora de Urquijo, who opened up her exquisite garden, the Palacio de Galiana in Toledo, which has made such an important addition to the book.

Umberto Pasti not only allowed me to photograph his garden in Tangier, but drove me to Rabat and extended most generous hospitality.

It is to Christopher Gibbs that I owe the introduction to Umberto Pasti, as also to Madison Cox, who arranged for me to photograph Le Jardin Majorelle in Marrakech under most privileged conditions.

Mr Mohammad Mir Mohammadi of the Iranian Embassy in London was largely responsible for the visas that Monty Don and I were given to photograph and film in Iran, and I am particularly indebted to my friend, Jon Snow, who introduced me to Mr Mohammadi.

I am grateful to Mr Ömer Koç who was extremely helpful in Istanbul, and also to Oliver Hoare who was most generous in sharing some of his experiences in Iran.

Brent Wallace's brilliant post-production work has, as always, been invaluable.

Derry Moore